TEEN GIRLS ANXIETY
SURVIVAL GUIDE

10 Techniques to Overcoming

Teen Girls Anxiety, Worries, Social Stress,
Academic Pressures and Social Media.

R ROBINSON

TABLE OF CONTENTS

INTRODUCTION

The world is not primarily created to accommodate pains, but the nature of the current system of the earth has allowed the existence of pleasure to be a rare commodity. Thus, we need to make the world a better place without much complexity for all to live in.

I dedicated my time and energy to researching and providing documented suggestions for life challenges. This piece is written as an insight into what anxiety is among teen girls, the major causes and suggested ways to heal anxiety among teen girls.

My research was based on a series of interviews while writing this book. Most of the feedback I was getting from the respondents that anxiety is rooted in teen girls, mostly out of emotional imbalance, which is orchestrated by their wishful expectations at such tender ages, which often leads to a high mental breakdown that could lead to a worrisome outlook, abnormal stress in mind and body, and some cases, depression.

The above factors geared me up to write this transformative book in the form of a guide that will not only assist the girl child in dealing with anxiety but also help in providing a template for parents and guardians to navigate a path that will help them cope with anxiety for their teen girls.

It is also worth mentioning that this guide has done justification towards the reduction of anxiety disorder that has found its way to the topmost hierarchy of mental disorders among teen girls in America and in most countries of the world.

This well-detailed guide was written in the easiest diction that could be comprehensible for even a teen who can read or listen to its audio-transcribed version, as the intention herein is to create suggestive ways to provide help to possible victims of anxiety along with a straightforward guide to avert such cases among our productive teen girls.

More so, this guide is a collection of documented studies in the public domain that will aid teachers in high schools to understand some psychological roles to play when they encounter teen girls in schools with anxiety as it has some elementary procedures on effective steps to utilize in making sure anxiety becomes manageable and minimal in our generation and beyond.

Although this is a transformative guide for teen girls, adults with anxiety issues can get some helpful tips to help them overcome anxiety. Therefore, it is lucid enough for any reader of this guide to digest it as a daily testament, for it is pretty educational, fun to read and quite insightful for anyone dealing with anxiety.

I wish to state that anxiety is primarily a state of mind and not a contagious ailment. Hence, it is worth knowing more about such a state as sometimes what we tend to see as a negative thought could possess its positive side beyond our comprehension.

Deer reader, I will encourage you to read this guide with a mind full of expectations because the tips and strategies in this book were tailored for you to overcome anxiety as a teen and thrive and succeed as a happy and worry-free teen. Happy reading.

CHAPTER 1

EARLY STAGE OF ANXIETY IN TEENAGE GIRLS

The teenage age is an age that has some modifications in the body of a girl child. It is an age that is preoccupied with questions based on curiosity about the sudden development that characterizes the puberty age in a girl child. These changes often affect the girl's psychology, who tends to be anxious and worried about being accepted by her peers in school and society at large.

In most cases, these teen girls tend to fear their next line of activity, whether it will result in praise or disappointment: a good example is the presence of low self-confidence noticeable in a teenage girl who is having her first date or, a teenage girl who has been asked to speak at a podium for the first time might be too nervous during preparation for such novel duty, she finds herself.

The quest to perform exceptionally well could lead to anxiety if not managed well. Anxiety is so common among teenage girls that irrational fears can envelop them, and a past event they have witnessed or experienced can bring them down.

Most teen girls tend to find answers to rapid change experiences at this stage, and if they can't find the answers they seek, they could develop mental stress that can lead to anxiety.

Anxiety has been rated to be the apex of all mental health conditions in the world. It has been said that about 40 million grown-ups suffer from it. About 25% of teens between the ages of 13 and 18 have been said to be victims of Anxiety Disorder. These statistics were documented from the research conducted by the Anxiety and Depression Association (ADAA), which shows that the average teen girl also has her share of worries over so many things perceived as challenges to them.

It could be changing hormones/puberty, academic challenges, efforts to adapt to a new environment, or even peer pressures. Most times, anxiety sets in out of stress borne out of academic stress, peer pressure, finance and rapid change in hormones.

What these indicate is that it is an arduous task to proffer solutions to every problem of anxiety using one answer, except one has a full grasp of what has led to such a state in a teenage girl.

It becomes more challenging when you are dealing with teen girls whose anxiety was caused by isolation or separation from their peers, as research from therapists who are professionals in this field has made us know that such girls tend to bear the pain in silence rather than open to people for support.

For a better understanding, I will talk more about the different types of anxiety, how they manifest in teenage girls and how parents and caregivers can identify the signs of anxiety in teenage girls.

MILD ANXIETY

Just as the name implies, it is an anxiety most common and easy to manage among people, especially teenage girls. Almost everyone, at one point or another, has experienced this anxiety.

Some therapists have even mentioned it as a form of anxiety with a positive side. Although disruptive, it has some elements of self-motivation for the victim, depending on the origin of such anxiety on the individual.

Typical examples of mild anxiety are teenage girls scared of tests or exams, whether the questions will be challenging or easy. They become worried and anxious as they wait for the result of the test/exam.

A teenage girl whose state of mind makes her perceive that she has worn the wrong make-up after she has stepped out of her house may become worried, which can lead to mild anxiety.

Therapists have stipulated that mild anxiety is mostly temporary but quicker to reoccur in different stages of life. An excellent positive side to mild anxiety is that it could lead to motivation and success. For instance, a teenage girl scared of failing a prospective examination might increase her reading capacity, aiding her during the test.

Also, a teenage girl who understands that she will be speaking in a debate might go to extra lengths to research the topic to excel in the debate; this motivates her to study more, which might produce maximum results, especially when prizes are to be won.

Hence, such positive anxiety has been referred to as Eustress. One peculiar thing about mild anxiety is that it is easy to manage as it does not have absolute control over the victim's mind. It might come with worry or fidgeting, or even the victim could notice a trembling sense.

All these signs are normal because the body is reacting to a sense of being worried or nervous.

Unlike other stages of anxiety, which are presumed to be a bit more complex, mild anxiety is an anxiety that humans quickly forget. So, teen girls can control them.

They can either allow the present cause of the anxiety to take over their happiness or engage in an activity that will arouse an elated mind since mild anxiety does not necessarily lead to a threat to the victim's breakdown of mental health.

MODERATE ANXIETY

There comes a point in an individual's life when they become too anxious or worried over an affair. It could be an accumulation of stress due to a missing item or lack of concentration or focus because of a sense of awareness that things are going towards the wrong direction.

Teenage girls have such disorders in a higher percentage than their opposite gender because of many factors, which often lead to worries. During their teen years, most teenage girls tend to pass through or face many uncertainties, which makes them more worried or fearful.

An excellent example besides puberty and its effects on the girl child is a teenager constantly worrying about misplacing her stuff. Moderate anxiety, on most occasions, is a result of the stress the victims of this anxiety undergo during an event. For example, a teenage girl who meets with a sadistic lecturer during a class presentation might quickly become a victim of moderate anxiety.

Bumping into traffic that leads to a teen arriving at a conference when it has passed her period to present a paper might push her into moderate anxiety, especially when she flashes back to the preparations she has carried out before such a conference but can no longer participate in the presentation.

This type of anxiety has more signs or symptoms than mild anxiety. It is noteworthy to state that there are positive sides to this kind of anxiety since the victim can still process ideas or communicate very well. She can even proffer solutions to challenges, but the place of utmost concern is their lack of focus, which Professional Therapists have identified as moderate anxiety.

Common signs of moderate anxiety include:

- Body pains
- Sweating,
- Anger
- Nausea

Moderate anxiety is said to rise to a higher stage of anxiety if not effectively managed. Thus, it is advised that teen girls prepare themselves against that by learning more about the cause of their support and seeking help.

SEVERE ANXIETY

As the name implies, severe anxiety is anxiety that has gone beyond normal anxiety. It can be said to be an anxiety that needs proper understanding and therapy to manage. Severe anxiety is more complex than the two other types mentioned earlier because of its hazardous effect on the victim's body and the worry and stress for the teen girl and those around them.

Severe anxiety may affect the day-to-day activity of the victim; as such, a person might have more distress, resulting in lower productivity and efficiency. Such anxiety may be easily detected among teen girls as they tend to show some signs which indicate that they are passing through severe anxiety.

Among these signs which may be noticed in these teen girls are:

- Inability to relax
- High level of withdrawal from their peers and loved ones
- Increased heart rates
- Nervousness
- Fear

A good example of the last sign is the fear of being appreciated and accepted by peers or the demise of someone highly admired or cherished by teen girls. This may lead to a mental breakdown and, on most occasions, might extend to the need for an external influence or care for the victims to become normal again.

It is worth noting that severe anxiety may trigger more enormous challenges like more healthcare finances and lack of happiness, which may result in sudden temper, fear and anger in the minds of the person going through severe anxiety.

Teen girls with severe anxiety see withdrawal from people as the best solution. But this is an unhealthy move since teen girls with severe anxiety need the support of family and friends to overcome this disorder.

PANIC ANXIETY

This type of anxiety is regarded as the ultimate level in all the stages of anxiety that human beings are exposed to. It is an anxiety that demands urgent medical attention as the victim might fall into depression and develop suicidal thoughts.

Among teen girls, this type of anxiety tends to manifest when they are exposed to a high degree of traumatic events that might lead to constant fear and worry.

Such events include:

- Rape
- Physical and emotional abuse at a tender age
- Witnessing or being a victim of a fatal accident
- Being a victim of kidnapping.

Issues like post-traumatic stress disorder, which is generated by exposure to or experience of a traumatic event in which dangerous things have occurred, might lead to panic disorder, and such cases could lead to panic disorder whenever the victims have a flashback of the events. The victims are often affected due to the fear factor associated with these events.

For instance, it will take lots of healing and recovery measures to make a teen girl believe in love if she grew up in a house where her mother was killed by her father during a fight that followed day-to-day quarrelling by her parents.

More so, a teen girl who was a victim of excessive bullying by her peers, which probably landed her in the hospital at a particular point while growing up, might end up living in isolation without friends. She might end up having a flashback of her past, leading to panic disorder.

So, a teen girl who has panic disorder behaves in such a manner that she might subject herself to daily worries due to her fear of impending danger her brain processes all the time.

Some symptoms that might be noticeable in a teen girl with panic disorder are:

- Excessive chest pains
- Fear and stress
- Short breath
- Abdominal pains
- Dizziness

Having classified the stages of anxiety, I would like you to know these anxieties do not necessarily change from a mild stage to a panic stage, nor is it certain that the stages will go from the minimal level to the ultimate level. These types of anxiety are progressively intertwined as they manifest among teen girls. However, there is a possibility of two types of anxieties happening simultaneously.

A good example of this is a teenage girl who is shy and worried about her dress appearance for the birthday occasion of her first boyfriend (Mild Anxiety). She might attain panic anxiety if she is asked to the stage by the celebrant to dance with him in front of a large audience. What this implies is that there could be a culmination of less anxiety to a higher level.

Furthermore, a trait that may be visibly observed in most teen girls with anxiety disorder is that most of them possess consistent worry and persistent fear.

While some therapists have also indicated the place of the gene in connection with anxiety disorder, some scholars have also opined that a more significant percentage of teen girls with anxiety disorder is a result of their environments as these girls are seen to be the products of their environment, such as every other human being living within the surface of the world.

For every stage or level of anxiety, there are practical measures that will help the victims to have a normal lifestyle, and for us to explore such steps that may be of help to our teen girls, it is also good that we know that anxiety disorders are of different types and stages.

A certain type of anxiety can be provoked even when we do not have any reason to worry. It is called Generalized Anxiety Disorder. Many professionals have categorized that anxiety does not have a permanent cure because it results from us being humans, and humans live every day with expectations, desires and uncertainties, which might not always yield the desired results.

Hence, this results in anxiety of different sorts, which might depend on how everyone responds to such events. Conclusively, I believe that the next chapter of this Guide will do justice to probable measures to undertake for any teen girl who is a victim of anxiety.

As you open the next chapter, I congratulate you ahead, which will provide you with ideas on how best to deal with anxiety, resulting in a happy state of mind.

MUSCLE TENSION:

Teenage girls experiencing anxiety may exhibit physical signs such as muscle tension. This can manifest as tightness in the shoulders, neck, or jaw.

AVOIDANCE:

Teenage girls experiencing anxiety may exhibit physical signs such as muscle tension. This can manifest as tightness in the shoulders, neck, or jaw.

IRRITABILITY:

Teenagers experiencing anxiety may become irritable or easily frustrated, even over minor issues.

EXCESSIVE WORRY:

Constant worry about various aspects of life, including school, relationships, or the future, can be a sign of anxiety.

MOOD SWINGS:

Anxiety may contribute to mood swings, with emotional highs and lows.

ISOLATION:

Some may withdraw from social interactions and isolate themselves from friends and family.

CHANGES IN ACADEMIC PERFORMANCE:

Anxiety can impact concentration and focus, leading to changes in academic performance.

NIGHTMARES:

Anxiety can contribute to vivid and distressing dreams or nightmares, impacting the quality of sleep.

CHAPTER 2

HOW BEST TO DEAL WITH ANXIETY WORRIES

Human beings are born with emotions. Sometimes, we are influenced by a particular emotion or another depending on our present mood. Some of these emotions could be disruptive, while others can be constructive.

Emotions might be happenings around us or provoked thoughts based on past events or future endeavours that warrant us to act or react. This implies that sometimes our emotions overwhelm our typical personalities. However, we can control the effect of a particular adrenaline impulse that tends to overcome our logical or sensitive selves as human beings.

Just like most emotions, anxiety has some effective procedures that can reduce its adverse effects on humans if correctly understood and managed.

Though research has it that anxiety is the most prevalent disorder noticed among humans in the world, it also does not indicate that it is communicable, which removes the fear of contracting it if one finds oneself in a position to act as an uncertified counsellor to people around.

Medical experts have proven in medicine and therapy that anxiety is not an incurable ailment and clarified that its victims shouldn't be denied the utmost happiness. This means that every human might experience anxiety and can manage it with effective techniques.

Given the above premises, you need to relax and reduce your anxiousness, as that is also a measure to mitigate anxiety in the body.

This disorder, which also has its positive side as a form of motivation that could lead to success when applied properly, has been identified to have a high percentage of victims among females less than 35 years of age.

Below, we will go through the effective strategies to help teen girls, parents, and caregivers manage teen anxiety and help our teen girls live happy and anxious-free lives.

Also, it is essential to mention that guardians or parents of every teen girl should apply all or some of these effective strategies to their teens as they will most likely look back to appreciate them once they understand life beyond teenage age.

Effective Tips to Manage Anxiety in Teen Girls

HAVE A POSITIVE MINDSET

Abraham Lincoln once mentioned that Ideas rule the world. Indeed, the good and bad things in life result from individual thoughts generated from different perspectives of human psychology.

This connotes that, as individuals, we are assumed to birth the offspring of our thoughts and beliefs. This is also peculiar to victims of anxiety whose thoughts and ideas might have developed this disorder in them.

Most anxiety disorder victims are likely associated with one problematic event in their lives or around them. For instance, teen girls who are sicknesses and accident victims might experience complex anxiety. In such cases, a positive developmental mindset can help manage the tensions to a lower level.

It is essential to have a positive mindset in all our daily activities, and even when the odds are high, we should retain positive thoughts and persevere.

Teen girls are at the age when they are most anxious towards most things: it could be worrying about their past experiences, current happenings around them or probably, the fear of what the future holds for them.

Such girls might be prone to mental stress, leading to anxiety disorder. It is, therefore, crucial that parents and guardians who have teen girls around them should endeavour to be their role models in life and to make these girls comprehend that life is in stages and that while they prepare hard to become successful in their daily activities, they should not forget that these stages have challenges which everyone must face.

Hence, fear and worry should be removed from their minds as these challenges are easily overcome without a negative mindset. Therefore, teen girls should relax and build their lives smoothly without reasons to fear and worry as they likely have higher chances to attain greater heights than those who consistently see errors and the wrong sides of life.

On most occasions, when teen girls are showing symptoms of anxiety, it may have to be a singular thought that permeated the mindset at that very occasion. For this reason, teen girls should maintain a positive attitude and shun every negative idea trying to intrude on their positive mind.

CREATE FUN MOMENTS

Life is meant to be enjoyed and not to be consistently endured. Chinese philosopher Confucius once said that life is simple, but we choose to complicate it. The ways of life were not designed for pains to overshadow pleasures.

However, humans have created their complex world, defiling those things that give them joy. Nonetheless, every individual is meant to be a master of their own life. Hence, what we allow to be our life pathway is navigated by our actions.

Similarly, like every other human, teen girls occupy themselves with worries and fears that affect their happiness.

These girls are often anxious about their needs, which might be material, academic, financial, self-image, etc.

These needs are normal human needs that lead to happiness but could reverse into anxiety when the finances or resources to purchase or maintain them are not there. Some teenage girls fail to realize that worrying about these things could lead to more problems if they do not cease worrying about them.

Over the years, I have realized that we do not get everything we wish for when needed and that not all aspirations or things we crave are achieved. Creating a fun-filled atmosphere makes us happy and distracts us from these avoidable pains.

Teen girls should know that engaging in positive activities or even listening to music that arouses happiness in them increases joy and positivity and helps reduce their anxieties.

Most people who listen to music see it as a way to either relieve stress or play it as entertainment, which may increase our adrenaline towards excitement.

Furthermore, parents and guardians should encourage their teen girls to complement their academic work with some moments of relaxation like watching movies (probably comedies or adventurous films) at home or an affordable cinema as these activities might increase their happiness level, which reduces their anxiety.

Yes, they may be curious, nervous or suspenseful to see each scene unfolding, but these characteristics will only climax to happiness as each scene unfolds.

Another way to make good memories among teen girls is by creating space for a beautiful vacation for them if it can be afforded. In the absence of a vacation, a visit to an amusement park can go a long way in ensuring these girls are distracted from the grip of anxiety to a complete atmosphere of happiness.

I will end this part by encouraging every reader of this guide to create a conducive atmosphere as our functionality and productivity level increase when our body responds to a happy state.

ENGAGE IN SPORTS AND EXERCISES

The twenty-first century is full of various sports activities; hardly will you see a single individual who cannot mention one common sport in their environment.

Sports have become so popular that high schools have curriculum periods designated for their students to perform their favourite sports. Besides those who attend a professional sports school, most schools run intra- and inter-competitions to give the students a form of socialization with their fellow students and build their students' mental and physical development.

One thing I have been able to decode is that these students are more proactive than those who hardly participate. They possess stronger mental strength and perseverance than others since they undergo training that teaches them virtues like patience, courage and endurance.

Teen girls should be encouraged or motivated to engage in sports, which can also serve as a form of exercise or a hobby. One of the primary reasons for this is that sports are fun-filled and have many health benefits.

When practised as a hobby, it can help lower the emotional state of anxiety, as these girls might find themselves happy and fulfilled.

For instance, a teenage girl who hopes to be awarded the best in sports might not be happy if she does not have it; however, her spirit is motivated by kind words of encouragement, especially if she has been trained to live every day of her life in a state of a positive mindset.

She can build on that push to train more, knowing she might attain that height one day. Such a teen would have gradually processed the spirit of never giving up and, thus, may apply such motivation to herself if she finds herself in tough life challenges.

Daily exercise may assist teen girls in having a relaxed mood. Exercise is generally good for the body, and it also helps in the following:

- Better physical and emotional well-being
- Improved blood circulation
- An avenue to socialize and develop social skills
- Bone and mental development

Regardless of their challenges, teenage girls should be allowed to engage in sports and should be encouraged to participate in daily exercises like jogging, swimming, skipping, or even taking a long stroll, depending on their choices, as they may accumulate so many advantages which will calm anxiety in them.

EAT A BALANCED DIET

The mobility and distance a car can cover in a journey may be due to the fuel capacity or diesel in it. Similarly, that car's longevity depends on the maintenance the owner gives her.

The sayings above also apply to human beings. The degree of healthiness of an individual to another may be determined by the diet and lifestyles they have adopted for each other.

A balanced diet, which is the compilation of meals with nutritional value in humans without excesses or reduction, might be a big step in calming and managing anxiety. Intake of a balanced diet may be associated with the body's bones, tissues, and organ development.

Sometimes, people with a low-quality diet may be full of anxiety, And even hunger may lead to anxiety in a teen girl if she does not quickly attend to the pleas of her stomach.

Every teen girl should be encouraged to take more balanced meals and reduce her intake of processed and sugary contents as the latter does not have the essential nutrients the body of a teenager needs. More so, healthy diets might help to calm anxiety, which all teenagers should consider.

LIVE A HEALTHY LIFE

During my interviews with some teens who shared their personal lives with me on what could lead to anxiety, I met a lady who narrated her story about how depressed she was during her teenage years that she became a drug abuse victim because she wrongly believed that substances such as depressants and stimulants are easy ways to eliminate worries or anxieties.

She narrated how she developed an addiction due to her regular usage of substances that were harmful to her body, but she had to go to therapy before she could recover.

Just like the story of that lady, many teen girls tend to see recreational drugs as an easy passage to flee anxiety. However, what they fail to realize is that these substances are working on the system, waiting for the real nightmares to actualize their purpose, which is damage.

The personal question all teens engaging in such should ask themselves is: Why should I be a damaged victim of another human's wealth? Every teen girl should desist from using unprescribed recreational medications as a solution or cure for anxiety.

Another significant element every teen girl may have to flee from is the wide consumption of alcohol since it may likely harm the liver, as daily consumption of alcoholic drinks may have been perceived to be one of the possible ways to destroy a person's liver.

As a teen girl, you should realize that your history or past cannot determine your future. Live in the present, forget about the horrible past and reflect on what made you happy back then.

Forgive that human or let go of that scenario that brings you that painful memory, and you may see for yourself that your happiness sometimes might have been hindered by yourself.

Don't be worried about the future. Keep following the right paths and look for mentors to help and guide you. These mentors have once been in your shoes and may be able to guide you more than you may imagine.

Dissociate yourself from peers who might make you inferior to them. Associate more with positive-minded people and be more open to people you can confide in. Don't turn yourself into a hermit because of fear.

Read more about your personality and temperaments to discover your strengths and weaknesses. Learn how to take a deep breath when you notice mild anxiety, and make sure you find an exciting hobby.

Lastly, develop the habit of sleeping well. I intentionally mentioned this as the last point as I have gathered that most teens with anxiety, most especially when they are in severe anxiety or panic anxiety stages fin, find it difficult to sleep well.

Inculcate the points listed herein to bring down those worrisome memories, and you may discover sweeter versions of yourself that have been waiting to manifest.

DEEP BREATHING:
Practice deep, diaphragmatic breathing to activate the body's relaxation response. Inhale slowly through the nose, hold for a few seconds, and exhale through the mouth.

MINDFUL MEDITATION:
Engage in mindfulness meditation to bring awareness to the present moment, helping to break the cycle of anxious thoughts.

PROGRESSIVE MUSCLE RELAXATION (PMR):
Systematically tense and then release different muscle groups to reduce overall muscle tension and promote relaxation.

CONSISTENT SLEEP PATTERNS:
Maintain a regular sleep schedule to ensure adequate rest, as lack of sleep can exacerbate anxiety.

HEALTHY EATING:
Consume a balanced diet with regular meals, as nutritional imbalances can contribute to mood swings and anxiety.

PHYSICAL ACTIVITY:
Regular exercise is known to reduce anxiety by releasing endorphins, improving mood, and providing a healthy outlet for stress.

OPEN COMMUNICATION:
Share your concerns with friends, family, or a mental health professional. Talking about worries can provide relief and foster a sense of connection.

THERAPY:
Consider therapy options such as cognitive-behavioral therapy (CBT), which can help identify and address the underlying causes of anxiety.

TEENAGE GIRLS AND ACADEMIC PRESSURE

According to E.B Castle, Education is everything we learn from the day we are born to the day we die. This means that we as humans are continuously acquiring more knowledge from the daily activities we engage in.

However, it becomes arduous for many people out there to be restricted within some boundaries of knowledge through new experiences they are meant to learn within the four walls of the classroom.

Acquisition of knowledge by students may be tiring, especially when these students are not academically sound, do not have passion for what they are learning or may not even want to attain higher education at the first instance.

No matter the reason for the unsatisfactory joy their minds are occupied with during schooling, the preliminary result most times could be a mental breakdown, which extends to a particular state of anxiety.

Among students who may easily be affected by academic pressures is the set of young girls in their teens. They may have been ascertained to be pressured due to various factors, including academic stress, peer pressure, inability to understand a particular topic, or even fashion sense, which they might not be able to acquire at that point.

The fact remains that you may never be able to decipher what is inherent in the minds of these girls at such points. Nonetheless, I engaged in interactive discussions in the form of conversational questions and answers with students from different backgrounds, environments, and ages within the teenage before writing down the points highlighted in this chapter.

I discovered that most teen girls shared similar reasons for being pressured by internal and external factors relating to the academic environment.

Some of these factors which may be probable reasons for academic pressures among teen girls are:

Low Self Esteem

As a guardian or parent, you may be surprised to know that most teens are victims of anxiety due to low self-esteem.

In my course of conversational interviews, one of the teen girls narrated how she used to avoid teachers and students who felt they were brighter than she was. She hated being called to answer questions and did not believe she could ever be a bright student. Her answer threw me off balance: she said, "Our family aren't meant for school; my new guardian is forcing me". I had to dig deep to know what could have been the reasons for her not believing in herself.

At this point, my curiosity increased, and I kept asking until I finally realized that her late dad made her understand from an early age that their family was not meant for school as their brains were not as sharp as the brilliant ones. I do not know why her dad might have made her believe so, but my primary concern at that instance was the havoc it would have caused her belief about herself.

She told me that each time she tried reading, she just stopped as she remembered that their families have lower brains that couldn't accommodate all she reads. Surprisingly, she asked why God created them to be different, and I had to intervene by ensuring she understood that all humans possess the same brain, which is empty at birth.

So many teens may be out there suffering anxiety about why they may not have some qualities their mates have. They may need help comprehending as fast as their fellow mates can understand, reading or writing fluently, addressing a large crowd in a debate, or even answering questions without fear of being mocked during class assessments.

Teachers may also be careful in always praising some students above others. They can commend a student, but comparing students should be stopped as these teen girls may have the wrong interpretation of themselves as they continue to grow.

The same goes for parents and guardians; kindly be conscious of the information processed in the minds of your teen girls when you speak to them, especially when they are little. Words like: "you are a dullard, your brother is more brilliant than you, I don't think you are meant to school etc." such words go a long way in bringing down the confidence level of these girls as they manifest more in their teens.

Teen girls should not allow discouraging words they might have been told to affect them academically, as they have unique characteristics that separate them from one another.

Hence, they should have the confidence and believe that they can do anything they place their minds to do, as that is one of the ways to escape from low self-esteem. Indeed, self-confidence may be the key to reducing academic pressure, as students who fail to believe in themselves tend to depend more on others to scale through or perform well during tests and exams, which might lead to academic pressure.

Learn from others, but never disbelieve that you can't make it with your brains. Do what you are scared of, like answering questions and not minding whether you are mocked.

Attempt debates and take a significant role during group presentations, read multiple times if you know that you are a slow learner, and always tell yourself that "I am a champion and will excel in my next assessments even when you did not perform as well as you expected in the last examination." All these will aid in boosting your SELF-Esteem, which leads to lower effects of anxiety.

Socialization Phobia

One of the significant challenges that teen girls may encounter is fear of not being good enough. This can be said to be evident in the lifestyle of many teen girls, especially when puberty sets in.

There may be numerous teen girls out there who share these same traits that lead to anxiety. The fear of belonging to the wrong caucus of friends, needing to be seen among the "biggest girls", or being known as one of the best fashionistas in school may be among the major causes of anxiety among teenagers.

So many teen girls out there are victims of anxiety due to the consequences of some acts done out of fear just to be accepted among their peers as top-class girls. More so, teen girls may fall into anxiety because of their lack of finances to buy jewellery to prove that they are among the affluent class in school.

When such teen girls seek all means to get money to buy these things and cannot afford them, they tend to be pressured by their peers to engage in illicit things to earn money. Sometimes, they may feel anxious when such money isn't coming as frequently, or the results of their actions become bizarre.

The fact that some girls are at an age when competition on who dresses well, wears the best perfume or even looks best among all may create a space of restlessness among teen girls as they may not be entirely rational with their actions.

The rate of abuse of substances may also be higher than at other ages for teen girls. Many teen girls may easily be lured into taking substances because of their anxiousness to ride with those girls who are believed to be "the celebrity group" in their schools.

This period may expose many teen girls to a state of anxiety as they may be apprehensive about being accepted by their peers if they do not have things they cherish much.

Teen girls should avoid comparing themselves to their counterparts or even the opposite gender since we all do not share the same background. Teenage girls should focus more on their Academics, let go of wants they cannot afford and cultivate positive traits that can reduce anxiety and worry.

Imposition Of Fear and Pains To The Teenage Girl

Humans are higher animals with senses that make us unique from other species. Humans have feelings that make us react to pains and pleasures. It then becomes an unfortunate incident when pain is inflicted on humans by their fellow humans.

It is an unfortunate scenario that most victims of anxiety in school are likely to be products of pains accumulated by bullying or punishment they may have been exposed to by either their teachers or their fellow students.

Bullying has been categorized as the most fearful experience encountered by students within the four walls of schools. During my interviews with some students, most of them told me that one of the reasons they might have experienced anxiety in school is bullying.

They explained from their individual experiences how they may have had to avoid some paths in school because of some girls who were always looking for who to bully or guys who might want to tease them wrongfully (for mixed schools) or even avoid attending some classes because the teachers of such subjects possess bullying tendencies.

As bad as these bullies inflicted these pains, they may not know how harmful their actions were to their victims. A lady slightly above her teenage mentioned that she seldom cries each time she remembers the memory of the beatings she incurred from a set of her seniors who shared the same dormitory. She said many of her peers later became bullies when they attained senior classes in school, inflicting pain on those who just joined the school.

The worst part was her mentioning that she still gets scared whenever someone tries to threaten her, as the system of her schools encouraged such. She said, "Whenever you report a bully to the school authority, it seems you have broken a code because every other senior will punish you at any slightest chance they found you making mistakes. Hence, the fear of being hated by all makes everyone fearful."

Many victims of such scenarios might find it difficult to express themselves when offended or abused and so lead a life of unavoidable worry as they are scared to mention such agonizing pains to anyone.

Teachers must desist from scaring students with each mistake they make. Some students may have developed enough fear due to how they get called out for every error they may have made in classrooms.

Indeed, a teacher might be forced out of anger to deal with a student, especially when the teacher believes that they have attempted every method to impact such knowledge on the student. Teachers may have to consider the place of differences in the ability to acquire a skill among humans in general.

They should be patient with these students and look for other means to teach them rather than inflicting pain through their words or actions. Similarly, many teenage girls pass through post-complex anxiety, which could be above the moderate level when they witness bullying and extreme punishment not necessarily inflicted upon them because their backgrounds or environment have never exposed them to such.

Health Challenges Due To Stress and Extra Curricular Activities

Generally, every student undergoes a particular kind of stress in the four walls of classrooms to other activities inherent in the school system. However, some students may not be equipped with the same passion and assimilation brains as others.

Some of these students might be unable to comprehend as fast as others, leading to worries about performing well, especially when their results don't align with their desires. This might make some of them always scared each time an exam/quiz draws closer, leading to fear and anxiety.

It may have been noticed that there might be a high increase among students who fall sick during or slight commencement of Exams. Many times, the pressures these students place themselves in a bid not to fail to lead to these sicknesses.

Some students may panic when writing their exams because they have been scared that a topic they avoided while reading later surfaces. Accumulated stress due to challenging assignments or tests and over-rapid preparation for an exam can lead to anxiety that may result in sickness.

More so, excessive extra-curricular activities like sports, academic clubs, or after-school debate and quiz practice may overwhelm the student, which may affect the general functionality of the student if not properly managed. This can cause body weaknesses and restlessness that may lead to anxiety.

More so, when teen girls are exposed to such extra-curricular activities, which most of them might be experiencing for the first time, the pressure on them might lead to headaches, pains, restlessness or even anxiety.

For students who have been accustomed to eight hours of sleep, it becomes a tedious task for them to emulate the system of night reading as some might be influenced to believe that it is the best time to read.

For some teen girls, this might affect their system most often as they may find it difficult to read at night like their peers, which may lead to stress and anxiety. Such teen girls may be prone to mental stress. Many teen girls who do not have the same sleeping habits might decide to do group reading.

Some teen girls who are just trying to master the reading system at night may likely be affected with signs of sicknesses like drowsiness during classes, feeling weak or even lack of concentration due to overthinking. All these may lead the students to perform poorly, which may affect the student's overall performance.

Furthermore, teen girls whose health does not demand that they indulge in tedious work might find subjects they don't understand as tedious, drastically affecting the students during and after school as they tend to overthink such courses.

Finally, teen girls raised with the spirit of perfection may tend to go over the edge once faced with strenuous work or discover that their results aren't great compared to those of other students in the class.

Teen girls should be discouraged from self-induced pressures. More so, teachers should abstain from creating fear in students whenever they do not meet their expectations, while the management of schools may have to come up with enforceable policies and actions against perpetrators of bullying and illicit punishment against teen girls.

TEENAGE GIRLS AND ACADEMIC PRESSURE

PARENTAL AND SOCIETAL EXPECTATIONS:

Teenage girls often face high expectations from parents, teachers, and society to excel academically. These expectations can create a sense of pressure and a fear of not meeting standards.

1

2

PERFECTIONISM:

Some girls may develop perfectionistic tendencies, setting unrealistically high standards for themselves, which can lead to heightened stress levels.

JUGGLING ACADEMIC AND EXTRACURRICULAR DEMANDS:

Many teenage girls are involved in a variety of extracurricular activities alongside their academic responsibilities. Balancing these commitments can create a sense of overwhelm and stress.

3

4

SOCIAL AND PEER PRESSURE:

The desire to fit in or compete with peers academically can contribute to stress. Girls may feel pressure to perform well to gain social acceptance or recognition.

TEENAGE GIRLS AND ACADEMIC PRESSURE

APPEARANCE AND ACADEMIC SUCCESS:

Teenage girls might feel societal pressure to excel academically while also conforming to certain beauty standards. The combination of academic and appearance-related pressures can be particularly challenging.

1

2

SOCIAL MEDIA INFLUENCE:

Constant exposure to social media can lead to unhealthy social comparisons, where girls may feel inadequate compared to their peers in terms of academic achievements.

STRESS-RELATED MENTAL HEALTH ISSUES:

Prolonged exposure to academic pressure can contribute to stress-related mental health issues, such as anxiety and depression.

3

4

BURNOUT:

The cumulative effects of sustained academic pressure without adequate breaks or self-care can lead to burnout, impacting both academic performance and overall well-being.

CHAPTER 4

SOCIAL MEDIA AND ITS EFFECTS ON TEENS

The 20th century had some significant innovations, and the birth of social media may be traceable to the end of the era. One of the tremendous developments that emerged in such an era is what may have been referred to today as social media.

Social media, which many believe to be one of the most extraordinary Ideas celebrated from the birth of the twenty-first century, may have created and also contributed so many impacts to the ways and manners the psychology of people living in this present era is, which is different from that of those who lived from the early last century.

It may be a thing of a general belief that social media may have led to more connectivity of the world, which may have led to an increment in the knowledge of others and their tribes through online conversation, easy transaction of business from any part of the world to another., example of this is affiliate marketing or even building of good relationship by groups that share same interests and like minds.

Social media, which might have led to so many benefits for humans, may have exposed a lot of negative contributions to many people, especially teen girls. Some teen girls may not see any positive sides of it due to some negative impacts they might have encountered in the world of social media.

Above all, one essential thing is that social media has come to stay, and its effect on an individual varies as the usage, content communicated by its users, and quality of time spent might be some factors.

As I said in my earlier statement in this chapter, some of the effects of social media are either positive or negative. To have a full glimpse of both, we should have some insights into how social media acts in both ways.

Positive Effects of Social Media on The Teenagers

There is no denying that social media is the future and has many benefits, especially for teenagers. Here are some positive effects it has on teenagers over the years.

Enhances Learning Acquisition

Learning is a continuous process, and the world might have gone back to the Stone Age since the provocation of the coronavirus pandemic led to so many citizens of the world venturing into lockdown.

Many schools have gone into online teaching, orchestrated mainly by social media. Millions of teen girls who may find physical schooling tedious due to the stress involved may have found happiness as they easily studied and acquired more knowledge from online teachers, mentors or colleagues.

Many students who are teen girls may have been occupying many of these disciplines depending on the subjects being taught, and they acquired broader online courses that boost the knowledge capacities of these girls.

This aids in refreshing these students as they tend to enjoy the approaches and mode of assessments during these periods, unlike when they had to answer questions publicly in classes, engage in the presentation of a topic or even be part of extra-curricular activities.

Thus, the absence of these activities while using social media groups to acquire knowledge may create deep happiness in the lives of some teens. Some parents have suggested using social media to equip teens with knowledge should be utilized more during this unstable period where the pandemic and all other related issues affect schools.

So, teen girls should be encouraged to use social media more for educational purposes that help boost their horizons.

Building Relationships

Relationships are a state of connectedness between people. Humans will not be able to build a great world if everyone decides to live in and work in isolation. Hence, the saying that no man is an altar of knowledge, nor is there any man that is an island of knowledge, also applies to teen girls who will love to connect for one reason or another.

The birth of social media has yielded more connectivity among teen girls with similar minds or interests. Some social media apps like Facebook, WhatsApp or even Twitter have brought people of different classes, tribes, or nationalities together without most of these people meeting physically.

Such mediums have led to many knowing more about other people's cultures, building a state of connectedness that transcends into business or emotional relationships. It is widely believed that many inter-country marriages have occurred through online platforms with the aid of social media.

There may be an increase in the mode of happiness and love when people who share emotional attachment, probably married, dating, friends, or family, are connected through social media, irrespective of the distance they find themselves. Indeed, social media may have orchestrated more output of Joy from teen girls to whom social media connects. Thus probably leading to a reduction of anxiety in these teen girls.

Maximization of Discovery

Socrates, one of the greatest Philosophers in Athens, was once attributed by the Delphi Oracles as the wisest man in Greece. In one of his quotes, he said, "Self-discovery makes a man." To me, a man in this concept may be generalized as human.

We may have to attribute many successes of individuals to self-discovery. Therefore, teen girls cannot be exempted from this idea.

While conducting a random interview for my course with some teen girls, I discovered that many teenagers could find their potential through their exposure to social media. A typical example of this happens to be a teenager who explained that she never knew how good she was in the world of brand promotion until she ventured into it.

She made it clear that consistently watching people who were into brand promotions encouraged her to do so. So many teen girls into fashion modelling, the make-up profession, comedy skit making, or even online marketing may have discovered these skills through consistent exposure to social media.

I came across a lady who made it evident to me that she could master her public speaking skills by watching those who are on TED TALKS. All of these means that social media space may positively affect teen girls if utilized properly.

Therefore, teen girls should be encouraged to focus more on positive social media content that will aid or prepare them well enough for the future.

Parents and guardians should be mindful of what their teenagers view or read when they reach their teenage years, as they may likely have a passion for such content as they grow.

NEGATIVE EFFECTS OF SOCIAL MEDIA ON TEENAGERS

While we can agree that the world has moved to the digital age and has many benefits, it has also done numerous damages. Let's explore some of them.

Lack of Focus

The use of social media may have aroused a significant deficit in attention spans, which may be because many teenagers who are exposed and ultimately used to the space of social media may hardly participate in an event without their minds flipping back to the contents they ought to be reading or viewing in the social media.

A good example is a teenager who might be carried away in a class by a friend she is chatting with. It becomes challenging for such students to concentrate well enough while the teacher is teaching.

You may have experienced it at one point as a teenager when you consistently think of how to engage in a challenge going viral on social media while in a serious meeting. Such may be evident because, as humans, we get accustomed to what we do all the time, especially when we fall in love with the activity.

Social media may have resulted in the low performance of many students in school. The obsession with social media may have led to spending time on it, thereby leading to students possessing laziness as a hobby when it comes to studying.

A teenager who should read at a particular time according to her plans might easily be carried away once she opens her social media app. It may be a gossip, gist, or even an activity of fun that may easily distract such teens from spending that quality time on reading.

Often, it may result in the student spending so much time on social media that a lack of moderate sleep might lead to Insomnia if it becomes a habit, thereby extending poor performance. At that point, complex anxiety sets in. Spending so much time on social media may negatively affect a teenager if not adequately managed.

Low Self Esteem

Teenagers' exposure to the social media world may be a contributing factor to their decreased self-esteem. Many teenagers exposed to social media might have been exposed to harmful or downgrading remarks that have made them see themselves as inferiors in society.

Teen girls who have experienced cyberbullying, which may be regarded as one of the worst things people encounter on social media, might find it difficult to believe in themselves or see themselves as part of society.

A teen girl who loves modelling and desires to become a model but has constantly engaged in a mental battle within herself and has self-doubt if she is as pretty as her female peers may kill that dream if she receives negative comments that say she is not pretty enough when she posts her pictures on social media.

It becomes worse if these remarks come from her school peers. She might never want to engage in any social activity again. All these may lead to mental stress, which may lead to anxiety.

For some teen girls, their expectancy to receive many positive comments or likes may lead to anxiety if these hopes are dashed. Teenagers may desire to belong and be accepted; hence, these teens may read meanings to most things.

Some teen girls may likely see themselves as inferior and unequal to their peers who might have such desires met. Also, the trends and extravagant lifestyles of celebrities, models and acclaimed, well-to-do individuals on social media may sometimes affect teenagers who cannot afford such lifestyles.

It may become challenging for such teenagers to participate actively in schools and other environments where they find themselves mostly when they notice such trends exhibited by their peers. The worry of achieving such height or getting those things may likely lead to extensive worry and, if not checked, may extend to complex anxiety.

Manipulations of Feelings

Feelings are emotional states that can be aroused by various communication or contacts. However, one of the easiest ways to evoke emotions in this 21st century, especially in teenagers, is to have good communication skills.

Communication is incomplete without feedback; thus, a good communicator can easily listen, interpret, and give soothing replies.

Teen girls may easily be manipulated by lies they hear from people on social media, and a teen girl is likely to fall for one who cares for her, gives her listening ears, and possibly provides simple ways she can indulge in getting what she wants.

A boy or man who already understands that some teen girls are easily moved by what they hear may likely create more affection for the teen girl to take advantage of her.

A teenager told me how she used part of her savings to travel miles to surprise her social media boyfriend, who claimed he needed money for his expired rent, only to meet the actual girlfriend in the house without the guy. She said she had to calm her nerves and begged the lady to allow her in as she was a friend of the house's owner, only for the young man to return and look dumbfounded. The rest of the story ended in pleas.

Another teenager explained how she told a lie to her friend and her mom that she would be spending some days with her friend. She spent these days with a guy she met on social media before realizing he was married with a kid.

Indeed, manipulations of feelings may not be only associated with the social media space. Still, it has also been established that social media has given more room for manipulating feelings. Thus, teenagers may need to beware of those with whom they share their thoughts, feelings and ideas and should not allow emotions to becloud their senses of reasoning because so many have indulged in some acts like:

- Giving private information or secrets to online friends.
- Sending nudes to trusted online friends.

Engaging in illicit or risky conversations with online friends may lead to complex anxiety or depression if they find their way to the public space through social media.

In conclusion, it is instructive to state that the impact of social media on teenagers might result in many things, one of which is a complete state of social isolation by those affected.

One of the biggest things kids of the 21st century might be exposed to is the lack of proper care by parents, guardians, or older siblings, who may not always be there to communicate with these teenagers in this "social media crazy generation".

The decrease in physical communication between loved ones and friends may have increased in this era of social media. Most people may achieve pleasure, fun, or a state of happiness by chatting with people they have on social media rather than with people they share the same physical space.

Do not be surprised if you see your teenage girl converse daily with someone she barely knows online than you, her parents, guardian and even siblings; the reason is that while social media might have increased her affection for whom she chats with, the real people she knew before exposure to social media might not always be there.

When those she loves and trusts on social media negatively affect her, she may isolate herself completely from others as she will not want to be a victim again. It may be fear of being victimized again or a way to avoid the memory of the pains she encountered that warrants her fleeing from the social world.

Those whose ideology about social media is to get support from others they could not get physically may decide to self-isolate themselves if they discover that they are mocked, insulted, or laughed at after sharing their stories.

Above all, we must know that while social media may have been a blessing to some teenagers, it may be one of the causes of self-esteem issues and anxiety for teen girls.

COMPARISON AND SELF-ESTEEM:
Social media platforms can contribute to a culture of comparison, where teens may compare their lives, appearances, and achievements to those of their peers. This constant comparison can lead to feelings of inadequacy and negatively impact self-esteem.

CYBERBULLYING:
The anonymity provided by social media can facilitate cyberbullying, which can have severe consequences on the mental health of teens. Harassment, exclusion, and online conflicts can lead to anxiety, depression, and other mental health issues.

IDEALIZED BEAUTY STANDARDS:
Social media often promotes unrealistic beauty standards, influencing how teens perceive their own bodies. Exposure to edited and filtered images can contribute to body dissatisfaction and the development of unhealthy eating habits.

PRESSURE TO CONFORM:
Teens may feel pressured to conform to societal expectations of beauty, fashion, and lifestyle trends, which can impact their self-image and self-worth.

SOCIAL MEDIA AND ITS EFFECTS ON TEENS

CONSTANT COMPARISON:
Social media platforms showcase curated versions of people's lives, focusing on positive aspects. Teens may feel left out or inferior when comparing their own lives to the seemingly perfect lives of others.

FEAR OF MISSING OUT (FOMO):
Seeing peers engaging in activities or events without them can contribute to a fear of missing out, fostering a sense of exclusion and loneliness.

POSITIVE AND NEGATIVE SOCIAL INTERACTION:
Social media allows for easy communication, but it can also expose teens to negative interactions, such as online harassment or conflicts. Positive relationships can thrive, but negative experiences may have a lasting impact.

REDUCED FACE-TO-FACE INTERACTION:
Excessive use of social media can lead to a decline in face-to-face social interactions, impacting the development of crucial social skills.

POSITIVE WAYS TO DEAL WITH SOCIAL STRESS

The world we live in is constantly in a state of flux. We are gifted with a dynamism that may have led to more results or solutions. In the contemporary age, technology has helped people of different clans to associate easily, and social media is an excellent example of such innovation.

This innovation, assumed to be the fastest way to share ideas, thoughts, and feelings, may have increased human turbulence and pains.

In today's world, it may be assumed that teenagers find solace in social media as an 'escapism' from the physical troubles of life.

However, this might not be true, as the same social media may have led to an increase in the happy state of these teenagers. Technology may have affected some teenagers as many of them may not share or discuss their challenges with their physical friends due to their exposure and dedication to social media, which often leads to isolation.

Most teenagers experience mental pressure from the company of friends they keep, family struggles and pains they encounter, or probably the unbearable side of academics they may be exposed to, which may lead to problems or pressure, which could extensively become stress.

Indeed, humans are an island, but we often become victims of social stress because we want to exhibit what makes us humans, which may be termed mutual relationships with others. These relationships may be in the business circle, academics, or family setup.

Social stress may have an outer side as it may be an external stress encountered by a teenager or an individual. Some people have opined that social stress is a stress that cannot be avoided, while others believe that it is natural, except one is a hermit with no single relationship.

During my research, many teenagers mentioned that social stress is a big challenge and that the environment in which they may have found themselves contributes to their development of social stress.

A good example is a lady who opened up about how she passed through social stress in her family as her parents were going through hard times and could not provide all she wanted. She mentioned that she had to meet another challenge in school as she consistently had to be a part of an after-school hours extra-curricular activity, which she could not refuse as she was among the best students in such activities.

It is instructive to note that social stress may lead to anxiety and, if possible, depression, as some teenagers confessed.

Maintain Good and healthy Communication with Others.

Communication is one of the most vital keys in life. Humans may be unable to transact and have a smooth operation if we find it difficult to share our thoughts and feelings. However, the kind of information we receive may determine our mood at a particular point.

One of the peculiar things mentioned by many teenagers and even adults whom I discussed during this guide is that valuable and good communication can lead to lower effects of social stress in any individual.

From the knowledge garnered during the interviews, most teen girls stated that their anger or lack of happiness that led to worrying resulted from the verbal abuse they were subjected to. A good example is a teen girl who mentioned that her teacher called her a failure openly in a class when she asked for an answer to a question many of her mates might have known.

In her remarks, this teacher called her a failure because she failed both the test and examination given to the class by this particular teacher in the previous year. She said this made her consistently fear asking questions or giving answers when called upon in this teacher's class and that of other teachers.

She ended up saying that this singular act by that teacher may have extended to the ways she could hardly express herself to others until she met one of her caring teachers, who she sees as her therapist and mentor because she always had positive words for every occasion and thus made her believe in herself again.

Avoid Negative-Minded People

Exposure to disheartening information, gloomy happenings, and various heartbreaking information or scenes teen girls are exposed to mostly on social media may have increased social stress among teenage girls.

Dissemination of negative information like mass shootings in schools, rising unemployment and even the pandemic may have incurred more fear and worry in teen girls.

Most researchers have shown that teen girls are more prone to have anxiety than boys of the same age. However, most teen girls interviewed made me understand that the occasional reports of the pandemic made them as scared as the most difficult-to-watch part of a horror movie, which made some feel that the world was already on the brink of collapse.

A few of these teenagers mentioned that they created a safe space and lack of worry for themselves when they attempted to shut down the avenues of such information getting to them as they engaged in things of interest, like watching movies with good content, listening to soothing music or engaging in fun games with the members of their families or friends depending on where the lockdown found them.

It may sound hilarious, but a teenager mentioned that she had to mute most of her friends who were constantly posting the news of contracted victims of the virus and those who even went to the point of showing these videos of dead victims on their timelines to her inbox or direct message were muted. She said she discovered that watching comedies while she read her books helped her sanity, which showed in her academic results.

Most teenagers also made it evident that negative words get to them, and this can be linked to research, which states that girls are designed biologically to be moved by what they hear.

Finally, a teenager also narrated how she saw failing a subject as normal. She said that her uncle was not worried about why she failed but focused more on the provisions of her schooling with a clause, "Your mom hardly passed too; I just wish you pass to the other class as you are not intelligent enough to pass well." Such words made her have a low esteem of herself, which affected her psychologically.

Some teen girls may have been experiencing an inner worry borne out of negative information they have processed into their brains that needs unlearning if possible.

Build a Strong Network of Like-Minds

Social stress results from external influences, which could be from those we share relationships with within an environment such as school, family, or even the religious environment. It then becomes imperative that teenagers are likely affected negatively when they belong to circles that give them more worries and pains.

A toxic relationship may lead to anxiety among teen girls, as some have mentioned that they become unhappy when they find pains in what ought to be a pleasure.

A teen girl may likely be angry if she finds herself in a circle of friends who mostly love attending night parties while her guardians do not allow her to participate in such risky parties. She may dislike such a guardian, especially if her friend makes her believe she is being treated like a kid.

The place of peer pressure and influence may be a concern when it comes to issues of social stress. Teen girls may need to build a fortress in friends by joining friends with similar interests. By so doing, they may reduce the effect of social stress.

A teenager mentioned that the best way to reduce social stress is by contacting her 'spice girls'. She said her friends decided to adopt the name of their favourite childhood female group singers because they act as spies to one another once any of them is on edge.

This strategy is an excellent way to establish a good network of friends. Having a social support network of friends and family has been said to provide more comfort and quick aid to issues of social stress among teenagers.

You may effectively reduce social stress if you maintain a group of positive and good friends who support one another, unlike finding yourself among friends with different opinions, interests, habits and principles.

Teen girls may engage with positive friends who do not appreciate failure, encouraging one another to succeed. Such platforms may lead to more happiness when a teenager starts and sees support from her members in a new activity; she may find herself achieving more, rather than if such a teenager finds herself in a group that consistently mocks at any form of error or mistake expressed by a member.

Arrange a Day-to-Day Activity in your Diary.

Most teenagers understand the effect of a disorganized day or a day lived by unplanned activity. They know that it can lead to anxiety and social stress.

A particular teenager said she was constantly overthinking her day, what needed her time, and how she was used to forgetting some essential things that should be done during the day, which occasionally affected her relationships with others. She stated, "I started enjoying heaven on earth when I followed my diary according to events of the next day at each eve of the day or sometimes a week before another week of execution."

Another added that nothing makes the day easier than knowing all your activities are meant to be executed accordingly.

Social stress may be lowered if the tension of not satisfying our daily tasks is met or known. But waiting for execution rather than impromptu activity pumping up our brains when they are close to the time of execution may lead to anxiety.

Teenagers may likely need to adopt this method of penning down their needs, plans, and goals in the order they may need them for execution, which may lead to the calmness of the mind and body.

Lead a Healthy Life

There is a famous saying that health is wealth, and a good meal distances the doctor for another day. Sometimes, teenagers' problems or the high rise of social stress may result from their engagements.

Dealing with people who are negative-minded, involved in physical or online groups constantly bringing down the self-esteem and pride of teen girls, or even indulging in acts that lead to fear or lack of peace may all be termed an unhealthy life.

More so, lack of sleep due to external engagements, lack of healthy and nutritional meals, or even engaging in extraordinarily tedious and tiring activity may all be categorized as leading a life devoid of good health.

While most teenagers made it a point of clarification that indulging in exercises, probably with friends or alone at some points, helped in reducing social stress, some other teens mentioned that they were involved more in taking a nap with soothing relaxation songs to ease anxiety and social stress.

Healthy living might be an excellent recipe for reducing social stress among teenagers. Regular exercises are a good way to reduce anxiety as they trigger the release of an endorphin rush, which may lead to happiness and longevity.

Exercises such as yoga help in mental relaxation, and visitation to spa and massage therapy and involvement in activities like singing and dancing may boost self-esteem and reduce social anxiety.

POSITIVE WAYS TO DEAL WITH SOCIAL STRESS

MINDFULNESS AND RELAXATION TECHNIQUES:

Practices such as deep breathing, meditation, and progressive muscle relaxation can help calm the mind and reduce the physiological effects of stress.

PHYSICAL ACTIVITY:

Regular exercise has been shown to alleviate stress by releasing endorphins, improving mood, and providing a healthy outlet for built-up tension.

HOBBIES AND CREATIVE OUTLETS:

Engaging in activities that bring joy, such as art, music, or writing, can serve as a positive distraction and help individuals unwind.

ASSERTIVENESS TRAINING:

Learning to express thoughts and feelings assertively, rather than passively or aggressively, can contribute to healthier interpersonal relationships and reduce social stress.

POSITIVE WAYS TO DEAL WITH SOCIAL STRESS

ACTIVE LISTENING:

Developing active listening skills fosters better understanding in social interactions and can enhance communication, reducing misunderstandings and conflicts.

CONNECT WITH OTHERS:

Building and maintaining positive relationships can provide emotional support during challenging times. A supportive social network helps individuals feel understood and less isolated.

SEEK PROFESSIONAL HELP:

If social stress becomes overwhelming, seeking guidance from a therapist or counselor can offer valuable insights and coping strategies.

CULTIVATE SELF-COMPASSION:

Developing self-compassion involves treating oneself with kindness and understanding, especially in moments of stress or perceived failure.

CHAPTER 6

COPING WITH
ANXIOUS THOUGHTS

Anxious thoughts may be referred to as thoughts borne out of psychological and emotional overwhelm, which may be out of fear, worry or any emotional state that leads to restlessness. Anxiousness is a state every individual gets to at one point or another.

During my interaction with some teenagers, most of them mentioned that they cannot but agree that anxious thoughts are one thing that needs utmost attention as thoughts may lead to any other state in an individual.

Abraham Lincoln once said that Ideas rule the world. That may be inferred as the positive powers of thoughts. The same may apply to the product of negative thoughts in an individual.

It boils down to what REMEZ SASSON termed mind power. The state of happiness, unhappiness, success and failures, victory and defeat may be regarded as the sheer product of the thoughts generated by our minds.

Thoughts are invisible; thus, what we imbibe into our brains and minds leads to what we express in words and actions. The power of thinking is one of the most incredible powers in life, which can lead to many disruptive and constructive creations by humans.

Anxious thoughts are likely borne out of fear, worry, distress, expectation, etc., and may lead to a complex anxiety disorder if not managed well.

We may have had results from people who were rushed to the hospital even after hearing positive news. A good example is a teen boy who said he fainted when his favourite football team scored a goal in the last minute of the match.

He said he did not know the excitement rush that made him jump and fall on his head. Though he later confessed that he had gambled with some of his colleagues on the outcome of the match, he was saved by that goal in the last minute.

I am not sharing this news to encourage gambling but to tell all readers of this guide that a surprise or even an over-exciting of information could lead to Severe Panic Disorder.

Anxious thoughts are any form of thought that is operated on or undergoes a kind of emotional imbalance at that point of thinking or afterwards.

A research study highlighted that stress hormones like adrenaline or cortisol are released when humans are stressed or anxious. These hormones cause physical symptoms like increased sweating or heart rate.

Effective Coping Strategies to Help Teen Girls Overcome Anxious Thoughts

1. Listen to Soothing and Inspiring Music

Before penning down these coping strategies, I asked a lot of teen girls what they use to cope with their anxious thoughts, and the primary response I received was that they listen to music to relieve stress.

Music is said to engage our brain's neocortex, which relaxes us and reduces impulsivity. Music can change our mood from a sad note to a cheerful one when we listen to soothing or inspiring music, and it aids in slowing down our pulse and heart rate, which may help reduce our anxiety or anxious thoughts.

According to Daniel Abrams, music boosts all brain sectors related to planning, focus, mobility, and memory, as dopamine is released when we listen to soothing music.

Music of Meditation has also been described by research as an instrument that lowers blood pressure, relaxes tensions in the muscles and may assist with improving cardiac outputs in the body.

All these may lead to the reduction of anxiety or even anxious thoughts because of the relaxation and calmness of the body. Also, dancing may be a top way to calm anxious thoughts in the body.

Arts of Psychotherapy explains that music can improve a person's mood, which can calm the body and help to reduce anxiety.

Music elevates dopamine and endorphins in our body. These two hormones, termed neurotransmitters, have been said to lead to high feelings of pleasure and excitement when released.

Some teen girls mentioned that they were members of a dancing team from where they derive pleasure, and at such points, they could hardly think of negative things or even be anxious.

The last relaxing strategy that teen girls emphasized was singing, which has more sensation of happiness. One teen girl said she had grown beyond anxious thoughts, and she hardly finds herself in such a state as she is constantly doing what she likes doing the most, which is singing songs sung by others or the ones she composed.

Another lady I interviewed stated that she does not like anything that will affect her happiness, so she joined her church choir, where she sings to people.

While some teen girls enjoyed music by singing it themselves, others loved playing one instrument or another for fun. The central idea generated by these teen girls is that entertainment and fun activities may be effective tools to cope with anxious thoughts.

2. Involvement in Works of Art or Creativity.

As a teenager, you may readily cope with anxious thoughts by involving yourself in creative and fun activities like reading comical or fun-filled content, writing a poem or anything you derive joy from, such as drawing or painting.

Studies have shown that fiction books can easily indulge the mind and create good imagination.

The human mind may quickly increase meditative qualities, which may assist the brain in concentrating on a single activity, which aids in stress reduction and increases relaxation of the mind and the brain.

Reading books is fun and inspiring and helps to hamper a decline in our cognitive skills. Some teenagers explained how reading their favourite novels, dramas, or even poems may have assisted them in coping with anxious thoughts.

According to Mancosa, six per cent of reading could lead to a sixty per cent reduction in stress in the body, leading to lower heart rate and blood pressure. These may help a teen girl cope with anxious thoughts as the body is calm and relaxed.

Furthermore, the time invested in writing a lovely piece or a poem has been described as a significant measure of coping with anxious thoughts. The Daily Telegraph opined that journaling about our emotions or fears is an effective coping strategy that helps calm our brains and re-establish our mental balance.

Studies have shown that consistent writing helps reduce activity in the Amygdala, a part of the brain associated with emotions and fears that leads to more productivity of the brain's frontal cortex, which is considered a mind regulator.

Some teen girls explained that penning things down gives a more relaxed mind as it aids in executing plans and activities they want to prioritize.

Journaling assists teens in managing stress and lowering anxiety, which leads to a maximum reduction of anxious thoughts. Similarly, researchers have described poetry as a soothing means to reduce stress, which can elevate your mood towards happiness.

Many teen girls explained how they increased their levels of confidence or how they found inspiration during the process of penning down a poem. Some teen girls stated how often writing poetry gives them the urge to open up as that is the most accessible mode to express themselves, which sometimes results in freeing their minds up.

Some even narrated how they have built up their self-control by making sure they write at least a romantic poem relating to nature or romance every week that goes by, which gives them something to think about and by so doing, they quickly feel happy most times in memory of the good words penned down or the new ones to pen down.

Most of the teen girls held that writing things of positive content or poetry has assisted them in coping with anxious thoughts.

The last phase of this segment is the passion or love for drawing or painting that most teen girls see as a means to cope with anxious thoughts. Most teen girls have expressed their interest and passion for drawing or painting, and they have seen it as an accessible medium to cope with anxious thoughts.

Research conducted by some therapists supports the claim that painting or drawing may lead to a high reduction in anxiety or even help teen girls cope with anxious thoughts.

Painting has been said to create a release of emotion, which may assist the human mind in relaxing due to the beautiful works of art these teen girls might design.

These designs may linger in the memories, and each sight of these stunning works may elevate the joyful mood in these girls and help reduce mental strains.

Arts is a kind of therapy that may lead to lowering the cortisol level in humans, which these teen girls cannot be exempted from.

A famous person who has also added her experiences in supporting this claim is Wardrip. Research has it that she has launched a support group for people with mental stress or acute mental issues in which conditions like depression and anxiety are named Creative Courage.

In her submission, she battled depression for many years, which made her start the scheme at the University of Montana with the name Creative Pulse. She maintains that art remains the best therapy to subscribe to for people with anxious thoughts, depression or any mental health problem.

In addition, studies have proven that skills like good communication, problem-solving, high emotional intelligence, elevated self-esteem, and even creativity may all be achieved by painting or drawing.

Most teens interviewed have been able to mention some of these, too, as they have been better off due to their exposure to the Arts.

Research has proven that creative art, reading and creative writing are all effective coping strategies to help teen girls reduce anxiety and overcome anxiety.

3. Engage in meditation and recreational activities.

Research has proven that relaxation activities such as mindful meditation and engaging in fun activities help to rewire the mind and, in turn, reduce anxious thoughts and anxiety.

Mindfulness meditation has been repeatedly illustrated to reduce stress or the effects of anxious thoughts in the body.

Some teen girls stated that mindfulness meditation helps them most, significantly, during examinations to calm their nerves with an improvement in their sleep when due, thereby reducing stress during these examinations.

Dr Weil, in 2009, stated that engaging in constant mindful breathing can assist humans in feeling relaxed and energetic, and it may even assist them in coping with stress-related health challenges.

Some teen girls may have supported these claims unknowingly when they described mindful meditation as an instrument to balance their immune systems.

Research also clarified that meditative acts like surrounding oneself in an environment full of nature or even watching and relaxing oneself in a domain or surroundings occupied by nature's beauties might give humans a clear mind as they tend to be more relaxed in such an atmosphere.

Some exercises may have some element of meditation, which may assist the body in sending signals to significant parts of the body to loosen up. Some of these activities are Yoga or Tai chi.

These activities are helpful in boosting self-awareness and may lead to equipping oneself with more patience, tolerance and endurance as the body may always be in a state of relaxation, which may slow down our blood pressure and kick against pains in the body.

Acts of meditation lead to inner peace, which can assist teen girls in developing self-acceptance and self-awareness when things go negative sometimes. With self-acceptance and self-awareness, these teen girls flow effortlessly with life, which leads to a reduction in anxious thoughts.

Likewise, recreational activities are said to be one of the fastest and easiest ways to manage teen girls' anxious thoughts. Some girls have highlighted that indulging in recreational acts is the easiest way to avoid being sad or unhappy.

Swimming, for instance, is one of the best forms of clearing one's brain of harmful or anxious thoughts. The soothing fun and happiness derived from this may easily cheer them up or boost their enthusiasm to engage in any activity.

Playing one's favourite sports may be considered the best way to reduce body stress. Most teen girls have confessed that the regular exercise involved with engaging in their best sports hardly makes them remember the negative parts or incidents in life.

A teen girl stated that she built her morale and bravery skills through her exposure to Volleyball. She mentioned that such sports made her understand that she has to win or lose in every situation, but at most, she needs to attempt it as that is the only clarification of the result that will later emerge.

She also described any award or medal, even a positive compliment received from others after every sport, as a way of encouragement. That boosted her mind to ensure she finished any tasks as that is when such honours are gotten.

These, she claimed, assist her in schooling too and have aided her from being too worried or anxious, relatively relaxed and calculative with the right strategy in all her engagements.

More so, activities like leisure tours to new environments and hiking are acclaimed mediums of having wider scopes in life and one of the fastest means to burn calories suitable for cognitive development.

Exercise, in general, has been elaborated to have a maximum connection with the reduction in blood pressure and flexibility of the body, which reduces stress and may lead to a high decrease in anxious thoughts in teen girls.

The next chapter provides insights into how to lead a positive lifestyle.

COPING WITH ANXIOUS THOUGHTS

STRUCTURED SCHEDULE:

Create a daily routine that includes regular meals, exercise, and sufficient sleep. A structured schedule can provide a sense of stability and predictability, reducing the uncertainty that often fuels anxiety.

PRIORITIZE SELF-CARE:

Ensure you are taking care of your physical and mental well-being through activities you enjoy, adequate rest, and maintaining a healthy lifestyle.

POSITIVE AFFIRMATIONS:

Counteract negative thoughts with positive affirmations. Repeat statements that promote self-confidence and optimism and shift the focus from anxiety to positive beliefs.

SET BOUNDARIES WITH INFORMATION:

Limit exposure to distressing news or social media content that may contribute to anxiety. Stay informed but be mindful of the sources and frequency of information consumption.

COPING WITH ANXIOUS THOUGHTS

GRADUAL EXPOSURE:

If possible, gradually expose yourself to situations or stimuli that trigger anxiety. Gradual exposure can help desensitize you to the anxiety-provoking elements over time.

TALK TO SOMEONE:

Share your anxious thoughts with a trusted friend, family member, or mental health professional. Opening up about your worries can provide emotional relief and perspective.

JOIN A SUPPORT GROUP:

Connecting with others who may share similar experiences can be reassuring. Support groups offer a sense of community and understanding.

MINDFUL WALKING:

Engage in mindful walking by paying attention to each step and your surroundings. This can shift your focus away from anxious thoughts and into the present moment.

HOW TO STAY MOTIVATED

Dictionary.com defines motivation as being motivated to act or having a solid reason to act or accomplish something. It gave a second meaning as something that inspires: inducement, incentive.

Similarly, Merriam-Webster. Com sees motivation as an act or process of giving someone a reason for doing something. Studies have indicated that motivation is the process that initiates, guides, and maintains goal-oriented.

While motivation has been explained in its literal meanings from different perspectives, motivation may easily be categorized into two primary forms:

- **Intrinsic motivation:**

Which has been said to be from the internal point of humans, that is, doing something out of innermost pleasure or desire.

- **Extrinsic motivation**

The second is the external point of view termed extrinsic motivation, which is an act engaged by external influences.

Create More Intrinsic Motivation

Most of the teen girls I spoke with during my research opined that one of the primary sources of their motivations is birthed out of their innermost desires or ambitions.

For some teen girls who find themselves within the corridors of an academic environment, they made it clear that many factors may lead to them being motivated as it may sometimes be tiring. However, one of such factors mentioned is loving what they do, which makes them enthusiastic about doing more.

In most cases, they confirmed that this zeal may have given them the driving force to engage in such environments until they saw the result.

Some teens also made it known that intrinsic or internal motivation may have caused them to become pacesetters in fields where they find themselves because of the dedication and commitment they input into any activity they engage in and not necessarily depending on people most times.

Some teen girls who spoke about their own experiences specified that the sheer fun derived from doing an activity is a better form of being motivated than focusing on external rewards that may be given as the failure to achieve the latter may often affect them.

One teen girl stated that she started enjoying the better version of her life when she understood the place of internal motivation. She made it known that she does not typically have worries, which usually make her full of anxiety since she learned how to focus on enjoying any form of activity she saw herself in rather than external comments, awards, or remunerations which are external.

The teen girl narrated how she became a good singer by singing her favorite songs often, which led her to want to know some things about instruments. She joined a choir and was always at all rehearsals, not because of the sanctions of not participating, as was the case for those who missed rehearsals, but for a single reason: to have fun and learn new lines and instruments.

She ended her statement by mentioning that within six months, she had unknowingly acquired so many instrumental skills alongside becoming one of the best choristers in a band of about forty choristers.

Such complements the quote that "Happiness is within." And it has been proven that people tend to do more when they are happy, which may be regarded as the best motivation.

Have a Detailed Plan and Follow it Strictly.

Most of the teen girls interviewed talked about the place of a detailed plan and its execution, increasing their motivation by having plans to follow their daily activities to annual activities. Some of these teens have indicated that the urge or passion derived from inner inspiration may have led to consistent motivation to keep engaging in these tasks.

Following the needs motivation theory, Abraham H Maslow explained that humans are motivated by their needs. These needs may be in a pyramid form of five levels in ascending order, where our actions are primarily motivated by certain physiological needs such as clothing, food, or shelter.

Most teen girls described their conscious effort to either wear the best clothes, live a comfortable life, or enjoy the bliss of the world in the nearest future may have added to their quest to read more, work hard, etc., and may have contributed to how they secure a detailed plan or goal to achieve such heights.

A teenager at her early level in college narrated how she maintained a good level of motivation in her high school days through her consistent reliance on enjoying what her uncle, who happens to be an aeronautic engineer, wanted.

She claimed that her uncle had described how to read and where she needed to focus, which made her create a reasonable timetable for her daily reading. She followed it up daily, leading to her seeing reading as a hobby rather than a tiring scheme some colleagues see reading to be.

So many teenagers described the art of planning prospective activities as an easy means to reduce worries and anxiety. They described the idea as a way to ease tension on what to do next and, by so doing, are motivated by the execution processes as they see it as a big goal to finish their plans.

Another set of teenagers asserts that they are easily motivated when they understand the task ahead and what it will take for execution. They gave their own opinion on what they termed an easy way to bring their motivation in any work, such as giving them a task or finding themselves in tasks they do not know about.

Hence, it may correlate with why students are given school syllabi to provide insight into what they may read even before the tutor touches it all.

Following up a plan may have led many teenagers to have an unwavering stance in their life when they are hit with hazardous challenges as many teen girls have explained during my course of interviewing them that they learned the acts of perseverance and motivation by consistently making sure that they followed their tasks to the end.

Attend Inspirational Events

Regularly involving oneself in activities that help boost motivation may be an excellent factor for teenagers to remain motivated.

Indeed, many teen girls have highlighted how their motivation level might have increased by their frequent attendance to seminars, programs, and events that preach positivity in life.

A therapist narrated how she has won over many girls who have reached the edge in life by making sure they signed up for programs where they are elevated with the right words, which may assist them to either follow new dimensions in life, have a passion not to relent in any career they are pursuing or find themselves being more committed to any activity they are exposed to which is a form of being motivated.

So many teen girls have been able to describe how they have acquired the spirit of enthusiasm and zeal to be motivated by being allowed to participate in events that inspire them.

A teenage girl narrated how she got introduced to speaking publicly: "I never knew I could speak well in public until I was assigned to speak on an NGO platform that deals with speaking against female genital mutilation; my discovery of my public speaking talent commenced with that single day of speaking."

She went further to state that the motivation she received from the founder of the Ngo gave her inspiration that has taken far as she keeps reminiscing on the words that the founder of the Ngo said to her that day, "You will be the best public speaker one day. Never relent in this field. You were made for this."

All these are the best forms of motivation for teen girls, as many of these teen girls have described attending events that boost motivation as one of the keys that may retain the right cause among all humans, especially teen girls.

Read Materials by Great People Who Share Your Interest.

A famous quote states, "Readers are leaders." This may also be in consonant with why many teen girls, therapists, and research works have indicated that reading may be a resourceful medium for humans to stay motivated.

Studies have exposed that reading inspiring materials by teen girls influences them positively, which is an excellent way for them to retain a high sense of motivation.

One such postulation by work of research states in a paraphrased manner that teen girls are prone to increase their vocabulary and communication skills, which may boost the confidence among these teen girls and, by so doing, may increase and maintain a high sense of motivation among these teenagers.

One teen girl who gave more insights on maintaining a high sense of motivation through reading explained how she had to start with knowing the in-depth meaning of at least twenty words in a week.

These, she said, helped her to be highly motivated whenever she was summoned to speak at public occasions or each time she found herself writing any form of write-up.

Some teens from different backgrounds also narrated how consistently reading books written by renowned authors in their fields of interest may have added to the wheels of motivation for them to achieve their goals.

While some may have seen reading as an easy way to relax their nerves, others perceived reading as a medium to acquire new life skills and information. Most teen girls have indicated the latter as a form of reducing ignorance of some ideas as they believe it is a thing of pride to accumulate as much knowledge as possible that many of their peers may lack.

Have Mentors and Role Models

Mentorship is one of the possible ways for teen girls to ascend the ladder of success and retain motivation.

Research indicates that the significant essence of having a mentor is to ease a difficult path, as one may need to follow the advice of professionals in that field or journey. Creating an environment of mentor and mentee relationship may assist in relaxing a teenager's mind as she may build in that activity; she finds herself with the sole aim that her mentor will always navigate the right path for her.

Many teen girls illustrated how their lack of a good mentor or one who can assist them by showing them accessible mediums in tedious tasks may have had a slow push towards some activity they see themselves in.

Some teen girls even went to the point of mentioning who and why they perceive some individuals to become their mentors. A young teen explained how she developed and loved Mathematics as a field of study more than other fields due to the caring teacher who taught her mathematics from a tender age in her early schooling.

The absence of fear or failure in most engagements these teen girls indulged in was highly emphasized in connection with their reliability on their mentors. As most teen girls stated, the sheer trust in these mentors may boost your motivation or make your inspiration comfortably situated.

For teen girls, mostly in school, mentors might come in the form of a teacher-student academic relationship where a student may find solace in understanding a discipline taught by a teacher.

Also, a lady in her teenage years mentioned that her best form of maintaining her motivation was sharing her problems and fun activities with her mentor, as her mentor had a good listening ear and would always offer possible solutions. She said the passion to be a mentor to someone someday also increased her motivation to equip herself with everything that makes a mentor unique.

Similarly, a young teenager highlighted how her close relationship with her five mentors, who are from different walks of life, may have contributed to her intelligence level, making her unique among her peers.

Create Your Own Time

Some people subscribe to only activities with the undertone of work without considering that the human body is like a machine and may need to unwind sometimes.

Teen girls must engage in activities that bring down the pressure on their bodies and infuse more pleasure. Many of these teen girls have stated that going to a Cinema, being involved in a sporting activity, regular exercise, etc., is an effective medium to boost motivation.

They made it clear that these excitements sometimes may have boosted their morale and motivation to do and achieve more. As some of these teens have said, having fun and inspiring moments is a means of self-motivation.

Maximize your available time, engage in fun and inspiring activities, and go for a vacation, as this will help teen girls learn more and earn such an enjoyable part of life when they grow.

HOW TO STAY MOTIVATED

SPECIFIC AND MEASURABLE GOALS:

Clearly define your goals in a specific and measurable way. This provides a clear direction and allows you to track your progress.

SURROUND YOURSELF WITH POSITIVITY:

Engage with people, enviroments, and activities that inspire and motivate you. Positive influences can have a significant impact on your mindset andenergy levels.

BREAK DOWN GOALS:

Divide larger goals into smaller, more manageable tasks. This makes the overall objective seem less overwhelming and allows for a sense ofaccomplishment along the way.

DECLUTTER AND ORGANIZE:

A clean and organized space can enhance focus and productivity. Remove distractions and create a workspace that promotes concentration and motivation.

HOW TO STAY MOTIVATED

IDENTIFY PERSONAL VALUES:

Connect your goals to your personal values. Understanding the deeper meaning and significance of your objectives can provide intrinsic motivation.

FOCUS ON PASSION:

Pursue activities and projects that align with your passions and interests. Enjoying what you do enhances motivation and makes the journey more fulfilling.

ACKNOWLEDGE ACHIEVEMENTS:

Celebrate both small and large achievements along the way. Acknowledging progress boosts confidence and reinforces a positive mindset.

LEARN FROM SETBACKS:

Instead of viewing setbacks as failures, see them as opportunities for learning and growth. Adjust your approach based on what you've learned, and use setbacks as stepping stones toward success.

TEEN GIRLS OVERCOMING NEGATIVE THOUGHTS

Negative thoughts may be defined as thoughts contradictory to positive thinking and beliefs humans may have about themselves.

Studies have shown that these thoughts may often be because of how humans perceive themselves, see things from their environment, or due to what may have been instilled into their brains from tender ages.

John Locke sees the human brain during childbirth as a Tabula Raza, an empty slate. He postulated that every baby comes to this world with a blank brain and that each baby is influenced by what it comes in contact with. Thus, each baby's personality is because of the baby's immediate environment.

Negative thoughts are explained to be the offspring of a chemical called cortisol in the human brain. Studies indicate that negative thoughts often may result from unpleasant emotions, unexpected happenings in the past, present challenges, or even fear of the future.

Some phrases that may be used to indicate that one possesses negative thoughts are: "I cannot win, I am a loser, no one climbs this level without failing mathematics, etc." These ideas or thoughts are like so many responses I received while interviewing some teen girls and professionals.

Research shows humans are unique based on their genes, environment, and upbringing.

Another point of knowing how negative thoughts affect teen girls may be termed the place of subconscious remembrance of a gory or dreadful event. Most young girls have seriously emphasized how an event that might have occurred in their childhood tends to affect them negatively in the present, or for some who are above teenage.

Anxiety disorder, personality disorder, excessive mood swings, depression, etc. All these and more are examples of how negative thoughts affect teen girls.

Below are The Effective Strategies to Help Teen Girls in Overcoming Negative Thoughts:

Understand Your Negative Thoughts

Studies have proven that identifying or discovering the source of negative thoughts is one of the primary measures to undertake in overcoming negative thoughts.

Research has proven that there may be mediums for teen girls to identify negative thoughts. Once these teen girls can identify the cause of their negative thoughts, they can apply strategies to change the negative words to positive ones and overcome the negative thoughts.

Below are ways that teen girl can identify their negative thoughts:

1. Avoid making fast conclusions

Many teen girls have expressed that how they envisaged a futuristic negative outcome may have affected their psychology on how they see life in general.

It is believed that teen girls who conclude something from its inception may be prone to negative thinking. This idea of arriving at an immediate conclusion, usually negative, created a shift in the psychology of these teens from a world of optimism to a consistent notion of negativity.

Teen girls may reduce their level of negativity to a positive and more optimistic one by taking time to process their thoughts and how such negative thoughts affect their brains.

2. Catastrophizing:

The anticipation or belief that events, activities, and occasions will end in negativity is known as catastrophizing. While highlighting points that may have led them to see negative thoughts, some teen girls were able to express more during the interview on how their exposure to vices or incidents may have affected them.

Some witnessed a vast level of directions pointing towards the negative sides, discouraging them from participating in events like school competitions, quizzes, sports, etc., to avoid falling into such a victimized position.

Studies have shown that people with such thoughts may easily back down from events they might have engaged in, which may have brought immense joy because of fear of failing.

3. Hasty and Over Generalization:

Most of the teen girls also explained how they may have had negative thoughts through applying negative experiences to all other occasions where they may find themselves.

A therapist I spoke with explained how some teen girls may have increased their pain levels by transferring the agony encountered during an occasion that is bizarre to each of their present day.

A teen girl mentioned that she rarely attended anything that was done at night. Be it a party, vigil, or even family reunion because how she had thought that anything done at night, be it legal or illegal, was immoral and uncalled for. The ability to completely let go and move on with all these personal pains, regrets, or Fears may be an excellent way to avoid such thoughts.

She ended this part of the interview by saying that her way of thinking changed when she went to college and joined a fellowship where she later became head of a unit and had to always attend night vigil with her colleagues at some point.

4. Labelling:

Labeling is defined as stereotypes that may become overgeneralized or inaccurate. This may be an extract of goals that were not achievable in the past or a self-limiting thought of oneself not being able to reach a height or excel in an activity.

A perfect example is a teen girl who explained how she consistently failed physics class because she believed she could never pass. Her story was that she was saved by one of her cousins who loved reading and was good at physics. He helped her conquer her fears by making sure he made her love the subject first and then gave her easy ways to study Physics.

Exchange Your Negative Thoughts with Positive Ones

All good and bad creations are offspring of human brains. That someone is either pessimistic or optimistic may be due to what goes on in the minds and brains of such individuals.

So many illustrations have been made by teen girls on how they may have improved in many dimensions of their lives by redirecting their thoughts from negativity to positivity.

To highlight this point, permit me to give a vivid explanation of some ways teen girls may exchange their negative thoughts for positive thoughts based on research:

1. Do Not Play the Blame Game

Many teen girls have been able to see themselves as the cause of their negative thoughts. Some of the teen girls I interviewed expressed themselves as the agents who orchestrated such thoughts in themselves.

According to various research, the easiest way to play down negative thoughts in such situations is to make oneself the therapist and not the victim. Ask yourself your response to your friend, classmate, or even loved ones if they came to tell you about these negative thoughts. As a caring friend or reliable sister to your loved one, I believe you will give them tips on overcoming negative thoughts.

So do the same for yourself if negative thoughts besiege you.

When you are faced with the belief that your actions strongly influence your negative thoughts, it is advisable to reduce such thoughts by applying self-compassion.

A hilarious indication of this is what a teen girl said: "I have no worries that get to me because I am the pope who listens and forgives my confession." She later made me understand that even clergy members are not always right and seek forgiveness from God.

So, avoiding the act of self-blame, thinking positively, and believing in yourself can help you overcome negative thoughts as a teen girl.

2. Maintain a Positive Environment:

Most people are said to be the offspring of their environment. The set of friends we keep may determine the way we perceive life in which thoughts are included.

BF Skinner, an American psychologist, asserted that human behavior follows 'Laws' and that the causes of human behavior are traceable to external influences. Thus, one quick way to replace negative thoughts with positive ones in a teen girl is for her to leave the space where such negative thoughts are gotten from.

When a teen girl may find it difficult to leave, active participation with such people or environment should be reduced. An excellent example of this was a teen girl who said she was contemplating suicide because her best friend always mentioned events in histories and movies where people who were famous fell or people who had lost hope in life had committed suicide.

She said she started reading suicide documentaries and movies that she did not know how such thoughts became embedded in her mind. So, her easy way of overcoming such negative thoughts was by avoiding her friend.

Another good example is a teen girl who narrated how she became addicted to drugs because of her frequent exposure to seniors who were into it. Hers was lucky as she discovered herself through another senior who took an interest in her.

Such illustrations and more given by teen girls may be categorized as mediums to exchange negative thoughts with positive thoughts. Sometimes, negative thoughts might warrant a teen girl to desist from a relationship or work in another environment, depending on what

spurs such thoughts in teen girls.

3. Embrace Journaling or Diary Writing:

Research has it that one of the means to transform negative thoughts into positive thoughts is to engage in the art of journaling. Journals are necessary tools to monitor your thinking patterns and perspective toward life.

Journaling can help you keep track of your life and make healthy decisions. It is a medium to record your feelings, emotions, and thoughts and an effective tool for changing negative thoughts to positive ones.

One renowned professional therapist stated that journaling, a work of creativity and extraordinary imagination, may assist teen girls in transforming their negative thoughts into positive thoughts. An example she gave is that of her patient, who was suffering from anxiety disorder due to her continuous remembrance of a gory event that happened to her in the past.

The therapist evaluating the teen girl noted that the lady looked calm and collected but refused to confide in her about what could cause her anxiety when she was brought to her office. She broke down in tears, looked terrified, and was asked to be taken away by her parents when a therapist asked her about her best holiday with any of her relatives.

The therapist quickly knew there was more to her story. The therapist asked the teen girl to pen down her life in a summarized manner in the past ten years to her present day.

Journaling helped the teen girl do some soul-searching. She might not necessarily be able to talk verbally, and the therapist was able to infer what could be the reasons for her anxiety, which was leading to her seeing life negatively and also providing probable solutions to the teen girl.

Journaling has also been said to assist teens who are constantly worried about the risky and unorganized lifestyles they sometimes lead, which may lead to these girls' worries and negative thoughts, to have a planned and prioritized lifestyle.

These teen girls may be able to have focused and relaxed goals, which may calm their blood pressure and may lead to them being imbibed with positivity rather than negative thoughts.

Improve your Immune System

The immune system is defined as organs, tissues, cells, and enzymes merged towards a single aim: to guide the body. They may be machinery working towards a single objective: the body's protection.

Research justifies the claim that the immune system may help you live longer if you have more positive thoughts than negative ones. One of the research projects that back up this claim was conducted at the University of Queensland, where research published in Psychology and Aging

indicates that older people who focused on positive information were likelier to have stronger immune systems.

Positive thoughts may enhance your immune system, as acknowledged by various studies. It has been explained that cortisol is a chemical that leads to a higher increase in negativity in the human brain and tends to decrease when humans have more positive thoughts. Serotonin is created when humans think positively.

The immune system is said to be a probable answer to overcoming negative thoughts if it is improved and enhanced by these healthy measures:

1. Taking Nutritious Foods:

Studies have proven that food with good nutrients may help improve the immune system. Regular Intake of food with a high percentage of refined sugar may lead to the impairment of the brain, which in extension may lead to an increase in girls possessing negative thoughts.

2. Practicing Healthy Sleeping Habit:

Many teen girls acknowledge this as a point that needs to be undertaken by other teen girls who may have assumed difficulty in not having negative thoughts, and they may have been relieved since they engaged in proper sleeping order. A good sleeping habit may be a bonus as the brains of teen girls are more relaxed, which may reduce the sense of negative thoughts in the body.

3. Limiting Late Night TV or Screen Time:

Stress may have been one of the fastest ways for teen girls to either fall into negative thoughts or have an unrelaxed body, which may lead to depression or anxiety.

Late bedtime, regular phone pressing, or watching the screen may hinder the brain's relaxation. Studies show that melatonin, a hormone responsible for managing the wake cycle of humans, may be impeded if teen girls do not find themselves sleeping on time.

Most ladies explained how they might have left the shackles of depression, anxiety, or negative thoughts by ensuring they switched off all devices one hour before sleeping.

Mindfulness exercises assist the brain in relaxing, which improves positive thinking more than negative thoughts.

In conclusion to this chapter, it is instructive to note that happiness and Joy are significant ways to have more positive thoughts than negative ones. Happiness is one of the swiftest ways to produce more melatonin in the human body.

Teen girls may have to erase the worries of the future and allow themselves to enjoy the present by following a structured system of optimism and plans. With this probable solution, I end with Dr Miyagi's words, "When you feel life is out of focus, always return to the basics of life. Indeed, no breath, no life".

TEEN GIRLS OVERCOMING NEGATIVE THOUGHTS

MINDFULNESS PRACTICES:

Encourage teen girls to engage in mindfulness techniques, such as meditation or deep breathing exercises. These practices help build self-awareness by allowing individuals to observe their thoughts without judgment.

JOURNALING:

Writing down thoughts and feelings in a journal can help teens identify patterns of negative thinking. This self-reflection can lead to greater awareness and understanding of their emotions.

COGNITIVE RESTRUCTURING:

Teach teens to challenge and reframe negative thoughts. Help them identify cognitive distortions (exaggerations or irrational thoughts) and replace them with more balanced and positive alternatives.

POSITIVE AFFIRMATIONS:

Encourage the use of positive affirmations. Have teen girls create and repeat affirmations that counteract negative beliefs, promoting a more optimistic and self-affirming mindset.

TEEN GIRLS OVERCOMING NEGATIVE THOUGHTS

BREAK DOWN GOALS:

Help teens set realistic and achievable goals. Breaking larger goals into smaller, manageable steps provides a sense of accomplishment and prevents feeling overwhelmed.

FOCUS ON EFFORT AND PROGRESS:

Shift the focus from outcome-based success to effort and progress. Emphasize that setbacks are a natural part of growth, and learning from challenges is essential.

HEALTHY LIFESTYLE CHOICES:

Highlight the importance of a balanced lifestyle, including regular exercise, sufficient sleep, and a nutritious diet. Physical well-being contributes to mental well-being.

ENGAGING IN HOBBIES:

Encourage the pursuit of activities that bring joy and fulfillment. Hobbies and interests provide a positive outlet for stress and can be a source of confidence and accomplishment.

SELF-COMPASSION AS A MEANS OF OVERCOMING PRESSURE

A certain teen girl has always believed she is her school's best athlete. She has attained the position of the best student in sports in her school. Then comes this eventful sports day, and she finds herself in third place.

She gets angry at herself, decides to stay alone, and even attempts suicide. Her family is confused, her friends are worried about her actions, and the other people in her life are shocked at what could have led her to such a decision or attempt.

She broke down in tears after waking up at the hospital and said she wanted to die. She says, "I am the best, and no one, absolutely no one, can take my place as the best athlete in this school."

The story above is a fictitious tale that may easily substitute for many teens who have prioritized their lives as the best or perfect beings.

Studies have shown that many live a life of self-confidence, but only a few subscribe to self-compassion. Besides teen girls, some humans have seen themselves as living beyond mistakes, being perfectionists or unable to achieve success, and having a negative mindset.

In many people's lives, self-confidence and self-criticism have been prioritized above self-compassion.

Dr Kristin Neff states, "Self-compassion entails being warm and understanding toward ourselves when we suffer, fail, or feel inadequate rather than ignoring our pains or flagellating ourselves with self-criticisms."

The teen girl in the illustrated story above has a strong belief in her potential and talents that she fails to recognize that she is still human, and as humans, we are not perfect and may not be the best every time.

All she needed most when she discovered her position in the race was for her to forgive herself for not being the best in the day's tournament and prepare for the next.

We may have heard about teens who tried to hurt themselves when they found themselves during or after agonizing events like rape, heartbreaks in relationships, prolonged stress, drug or alcohol abuse, or even a bad result in school.

In a research titled "Understanding the Relation Between Self-compassion and Suicide Risk Among Adolescents in a Post-disaster Context: Mediating Roles of Gratitude and Post Traumatic Stress Disorder" by Aiyi Liu, Wenchao Wang, and Xinchin Wu. They affirmed that self-compassion could be a significant factor in eliminating suicide tendencies among teens and young adults.

They indicate that self-compassion may be divided into two phases: Positive and Negative. However, they maintained that positive self-compassion might give the teen or young adult balance and a focused mind on the positive sides of life.

Thus, positive self-compassion may reduce the risk of attempting suicide by reducing teen girls' anxiety and depression.

They further explained that positive self-compassion might help a teen girl care about her feelings and bring down negative thoughts about herself, especially when facing traumatic or overbearing pressure.

In addition, they added that people with positive self-compassion might have low levels of post-traumatic stress disorder.

They highlighted an instance from Hiraoka et al. (2015) of positive self-compassion aiding Iraqi soldiers in overcoming post-traumatic stress disorder.

At this stance, it will be nice to expatiate on research points of probable elements of self-compassion as an avenue to overcome pressure among teen girls:

Mindful Self-Compassion

Kabat Zinn 2003 sees Mindfulness as the awareness that arises by intentionally paying attention, in the present moment and in a non-judgmental way, to the flow of experience.

Mindful self-compassion may be seen as one of the most effective ways of alleviating the high level of self-criticism, which may, in turn, lead to a high level of life satisfaction alongside a reduction in stress and alleviating depression and anxiety.

Jon Kabat-Zinn, who is known to be the founder of the Mindfulness-Based Stress Reduction Program, further reiterates how Mindfulness may assist a teen girl in understanding and expressing her emotions and feelings without being judgemental, while Chris Germer, co-founder of the Mindful self-compassion Centre defines self-compassion as the capacity to comfort and soothe ourselves with encouragement when we suffer, fail or feel inadequate.

To him, self-compassion is learned partly by connecting with our innate compassion for others, and self-compassion also helps to grow and sustain our compassion for others.

Mindfulness and self-compassion are coping techniques that can help teen girls overcome pressure.

Some Effective Steps on how to Utilize Mindful Self-Compassion are:

1. Experiment with Mindfulness:

Explore the preference in thoughts or feelings you indulge in when you see or feel a negative belief. **Ask yourself some questions like:**

- Why do I have such thoughts?
- Who or what propels them more in me?
- What could have been the major factors behind these thoughts?
- What was my location when such thoughts came?
- What were the words discussed at the location?

2. Examine Unfavorable Emotions or Thoughts:

Pen down all the thoughts you may have had in the first step. Develop your awareness and comprehension of these negative thoughts about yourself and be very familiar with them anywhere you find them. Try to merge them with the very beginning of their first encounter.

3. Accept these Thoughts or Feelings:

We often attempt to reject or flee from negative thoughts or feelings, which often leads to more mental pressure as our brain is in serious combat with these thoughts. Know these thoughts and accept them as part of your flaws. By so doing, you may see them as what makes you human and imperfect.

4. Avoid Self-Criticism and Forgive Yourself:

We tend to be harsh on ourselves against some errors or thoughts, opening a path for more pressure. Ask yourself your response if you find your loved ones having such thoughts. Would you be harsh or supportive?

Learn to forgive yourself the same way you will forgive that loved one. Be compassionate to yourself like you are to a dear person. Apply this to yourself, and you may easily get out of pressure.

Self-Kindness

Many times, we may be faced with so many challenges. We may feel that we are solely created to engage in such predicaments that we may fail to take good care of the body experiencing this pressure.

An excellent example is humans who toil day in and day out but hardly decide to provide healthy supplements or, better still, engage in any activity that will relieve them from the pains and agonies of these tedious tasks.

It is also a matter of clarity that, most times, people may provide answers or soothing words to friends or loved ones facing a particular problem but may also redirect those words to themselves in such situations.

The place of extending kindness to yourself in the face of challenges, pains, tedious tasks, or anxiety may be termed self-kindness. Self-kindness may be a natural phenomenon to those who believe in it.

Through my interviews with some teenage girls, I could infer that they may have been too harsh on themselves while having an easy-going or smooth-running lifestyle of affection and kindness to others.

For instance, one of the teens gave a vivid illustration of how she had been able to console her best friend when she did not make a good grade on one of the assessments. I asked her what her worst day was, and she mentioned that it was a day in her high school when she discovered that she was no longer the best student in one of her subjects and could not forgive herself for what happened in that session.

This scenario shows that some teen girls find it easier to be kind and compassionate to others, while they may find it difficult to extend such kindness. Self-kindness is a way to be generous or friendly to yourself and also a medium to ease pressure among teen girls.

Below are the effective steps to help teen girls develop self-kindness:

1. Extend Your Kindness of Others to Yourself:

Just like one of the illustrations given above about the teen girl who might not have known that she had a kind heart and affection towards her friend, whereas she hardly had the same for herself, many teen girls hardly find it easy to extend their kindness, and compassion or generous gestures back to themselves. We may tend to focus on making sure our loved ones are cheered up during crises, but the result may not always be the same for ourselves.

As a teen girl, it may be nice if you could extend the same feelings and emotions you apply to that good friend of yours to yourself when you sense any sign of pressure or pain.

Create or write down the memory of that moment you were sorry or kind to a close friend since this may assist you in having a positive image of yourself when you are down and need help.

- **Ask yourself: What would I have told my friend if she found herself in the same position as mine now?**

When you get your answers, you may apply such a sense of kindness to yourself.

2. Reapply the Same Kindness Given to You by Others to Yourself:

Sometimes, we may need a flashback or go back to memory lane to remember past happenings, and on some occasions, we may tend to remember some good deed that may have been done to us by others. It could be from family members, friends, tutors, guardians, or even schoolmates.

The probable suggestion to give self-kindness to yourself is to bring back a memory of a kind gesture extended to you by others. This may help reduce stress or pressure as the brain may refresh such a good memory.

An excellent example of this is imagine that big uncle who usually guides you through your complex assignments, and in the course of assisting you with such assignments, he usually makes sure you go through numerous and tiring examples and then works with you on probable solutions.

Such an example is a means to reapply the recipient's kindness to yourself by maintaining good responses or positive attitudes to external influences.

2. Engage Yourself with Soothing Words:

So many people may have been able to express themselves to others using humble and soothing words. The reverse may be true for some who have not applied such a habit. Many people may have used disheartening words on themselves, forgetting to remember that they are human and should be cared for and supported.

One famous artist named James Brown once sang a song saying he "feels good." The question that may beg for an immediate answer when we engage ourselves or go into self-conversation is: how do I feel? Don't I deserve to be happy? And so on.

Answers like: I deserve to be happy, I feel good, though I attempted all I could, I will do more next time, etc. It is likely the best and most positive option prompted immediately by the brain that may assist teen girls in overcoming pressure.

Most teenage girls acknowledged that they might have been used to pouring unhealthy words/statements on themselves when facing complex or pressured tasks. An example of such words is: "This is the end of the road; I am a total failure, and I can't pass Mathematics." All these kinds of statements may foster a negative mindset rather than self-kindness.

Positive affirmation words like: "I will be the best next time, I am strong and courageous, I am human" will help teen girls overcome pressure. Teen girls may easily overcome pressure when they apply this point of engaging themselves with soothing words.

Universal or Common Humanity

While some teen girls have taken isolation as their place of refuge, some may have found interest in understanding the stance of universality.

A teen girl who may have failed in an assessment or sports activity may feel she has hit the end of the road by suffering pain. Unknowingly, she may be one of the thousands of people who have failed an assessment worldwide.

Similarly, a teen girl who has just been met with a broken relationship may see that as the most painful thing. Little will she understand at that point that many have also experienced such and, thus, may acquire more traits like being courageous and confident.

Indeed, humans may associate pains with themselves when they are faced with bad things, which is often the case as many may believe that they have been met with the worst situation in life and may not understand that they are facing the same challenges that some other humans in some parts of the world may be facing too.

When humans, especially teen girls, have a complete comprehension of shared experiences, pains, suffering, and other feelings they have with other humans, they may know and understand that they need to have a sense of compassion for themselves.

Recognizing common humanity makes us understand that we are humans and have the same problems that other humans may be experiencing.

A good example is that a teen girl going through menstrual cramps may be relieved when she realizes that her friend or even loved one has experienced such.

As a teen girl, you will develop the courage to overcome pressures when you understand that your worries, anxiety, pains, or suffering are not reserved or meant for you alone; instead, it is a universal thing shared with other teen girls like you.

SELF COMPASSION AS A MEANS OF OVERCOMING PRESSURE

ACKNOWLEDGE AND VALIDATE FEELINGS:

Mindful awareness involves recognizing and accepting one's emotions without judgment. When under pressure, acknowledging feelings of stress or anxiety and validating them as normal human experiences can be a crucial first step.

CHALLENGE NEGATIVE SELF-TALK:

Self-compassion involves challenging challenging negative and self-critical thoughts. When faced with pressure, replace harsh self-talk with more supportive and encouraging language. Treat yourself with the same kindness you would offer to a friend in a similar situation.

RECOGNIZE SHARED EXPERIENCES:

Understanding that pressure is a common part of the human experience can foster a sense of connection. Many individuals face similar challenges, and recognizing this shared humanity can alleviate feelings of isolation and self-blame.

ACKNOWLEDGE IMPERFECTION:

Embrace the reality that everyone makes mistakes and faces challenges. Instead of expecting perfection, focus on learning and growth. Acknowledge that imperfection is part of the human experience, and self-improvement is an ongoing process.

SELF COMPASSION AS A MEANS OF OVERCOMING PRESSURE

PRIORITIZE WELL-BEING:

Self-compassion involves taking care of one's physical and mental well-being. When feeling pressure, prioritize activities that promote relaxation and joy, such as engaging in hobbies, getting enough sleep, and practicing self-care routines.

EMBRACE A GROWTH MINDSET:

Approach challenges with a growth mindset, viewing setbacks asopportunities for learning and development. Instead of viewing failure as a reflection of personal worth, see it as a stepping-pingstone toward improvement.

CREATE POSITIVE AFFIRMATIONS:

Develop a set of positive affirmations that reinforce self-compassion. These affirmations can serve as reminders of your worth and capabilities during times of pressure.

CONNECT WITH OTHERS:

Reach out to friends, family, or mentors for support. Sharing your experiences and challenges with others can provide a different perspective and emotional encouragement.

CHAPTER 10

THE IMPORTANCE OF ENDURANCE IN SOLVING SOCIAL STRESS

Every human being lives with what is called emotions. These emotions are partly why human beings behave the way they behave and react to issues at each distinctive point.

According to some renowned psychologists, humans are moved by emotions that may result from their encounters with their environments. However, these emotions may lead to some outputs that may not be good for some people as they might affect the mental state of those having the emotions.

More so, some humans may derive stress from some emotions emanating from external sources. This stress could be generated from our close encounters, physical issues, or the external phase known as social stress.

Endurance is one of the traits that lead to the effective reduction of social stress in humans.

According to Dictionary.com, Endurance is the ability or strength to continue or persevere despite fatigue, stress, or other adverse conditions. Also, Merriam-Webster defined endurance as the ability to withstand hardship or adversity.

On the other hand, as explained by Wikipedia, social stress originates from an individual's relationship with others and the social environment in general.

Social stress is more common among millennials (18-33 years) and GEN Xers (34-47). It has been defined to originate from words like verbal aggression from people of higher cadre or even clients.

One suggested way to reduce emotional stress is through a persevering attitude termed endurance.

Some of the Significant Importance of Endurance in creating Solutions for Social Stress among Teen Girls are as follows:

1. It Sharpens and Improves Your Brain Memory

Engaging in sporting activities is one way to acquire endurance skills. Regular exercise helps to infuse more blood into the brain, which aids in increasing endorphins in the body. Endorphins are neurotransmitters that make the brain feel good.

Some teenage girls acknowledged that the ability to endure while reading a book or engaging in a challenging exercise helped them endure the social stress they may have encountered many times.

A teen girl shared how she was persistently suffering from stressful engagements in school. She joined the sports team and was always frustrated whenever she was selected for top races until she started loving them. It significantly improved her mental focus and other activities as she learned the spirit of endurance whenever she was occupied with any task.

Whether the task was challenging or not was no longer her fear; instead, it was the mindset to make sure she finished whatever she started that mattered.

Another teen girl also mentioned how she became one of the best students of Mathematics in her school through her spirit of endurance in ensuring she acquired all the formulas and steps needed in any topic she was learning.

Many teen girls confessed that cultivating endurance through exercises like Yoga or even reading a series of books that may not be interesting but needed to be finished may have enhanced their problem-solving skills. Many teen girls also concluded that endurance may have assisted them in being more concentrated on a course.

Another teen girl narrated that her occasional listening to long, complex, educational audios may have aided her in tackling social stress as she mostly but not intentionally had to transfer her enduring nature when faced with tough challenges.

One therapist stated that she often tends to improve her clients' mental balance by ensuring they are engaged in activities that push up their enduring nature. In that way, most of her clients may end up seeing the positive side of life and also understand that whatever their challenges may be, they may only require them to take charge with more emotional and mental balance instruments through a cultivated endurance over time.

Improved self-esteem

Endurance obtained from activities like exercises can improve the self-esteem of teen girls.

Most teen girls tend to worry about things such as how they dress, reactions about their dressings from others, their daily academic challenges, body shape, etc. All these and more may tend to decrease the self-esteem of a teen girl if not adequately addressed.

The place of endurance in solving social stress may have been a significant key to improving the self-esteem of these teen girls. Some of the teens interviewed who shared their stories emphasized how the challenging activities they endured and survived may have boosted their self-confidence.

It has been observed that routine exercises that build more endurance tend to improve an individual's confidence in being victorious in any challenges that befall them. Studies have indicated that characteristics like fear of failure and pessimistic approaches to life that challenge teens may likely and partly be connected to lower self-esteem.

Studies have also ascertained that the physical way a person feels about himself may determine their perception and mental state, as well as how they react to things. For clarity on this, one of the teen girls interviewed gave the impression that since she gained the knowledge of endurance and understood it through practical experiences in tedious and strenuous activities that may have built the earlier endurance in her, she has developed a high sense of self-esteem.

She stated that she learned that anything that will yield a higher result starts with how one perceives it. Hence, she is consistent in whatever she comes in contact with. She made a viral quote among people who believe in Christianity: "I can do all things through Christ that strengthens me."

Her consistent finishing of all books, no matter how bulky and uninteresting they are, increased her confidence and enduring capacity to finish any task. She ended by saying that she has infused her brain with some ideological phrases she has learned through reading books, like "Human is the maker of all things. Things that are, are; And things that are not."

Furthermore, some teen girls shared their stories on how sporting activities like running, jogging, or even playing long tennis may have given them more mental strength, which may have increased their self-esteem.

One of the teens illustrated how her knowledge of abiding by a physical activity given to her by her gym coach until it finished may have led to her acquiring unshakable endurance. She said it was not always easy at first, but it became an everyday occurrence as she mastered the art of endurance.

Most teen girls also explain that their academic prowess may have increased by their high self-esteem, partly brought about by the acquisition of endurance generated by engaging in tasking physical activities.

Provision of Quality Social Network

Various research indicates that good and quality sleep is good for the person involved and the brain of the individual engaging in it. Studies have shown that aerobic exercise increases the quantity of slow-wave sleep (deep sleep).

According to Gamaldo's piece "Exercising for Better Sleep," 30 minutes of regular aerobic exercise may enhance sound sleep from the individual engaging in it. Gamaldo further explained that activities that boost endurance among teen girls, like active participation in yoga class, may increase the heart rate, which in turn may help establish the brain's biological processes that aid in quality sleep.

While many teens may have indicated that they tend to be on medication before they engage in a sound sleep, others have also mentioned how moderate exercise may have aided them in having a good sleep.

Regularly exercising has reduced the high risk of obesity and diseases like diabetes.

A teen girl mentioned how she could overcome her insomnia by engaging in challenging meditation exercises that led to more virtue of endurance. She created a good routine of her time for sleep, which she mastered for almost ten days before she got used to it.

She explained how she improved in many activities, such as academics, sports, etc., by transferring the power she got from the therapeutic effect of good sleep to every other engagement in which she involved herself.

Studies have established that between 8 and 10 hours of sleep daily improves the brain's rejuvenation and performance. It further explains that such a sleeping pattern prevents brain impairment and keeps it refreshing.

Endurance obtained from physical activity, which assists in reducing social stress, may enhance good mental development, leading to stable and balanced sleeping among teen girls. Some teen girls also mentioned how consistently indulging in physical activity in time may have provided them with the best sleep, resulting in their activeness in all activities they are exposed to, whether strenuous or challenging.

Enforcement of a Reliable Social Network

Friendships are most appreciated when people of like minds come together.

Research has proven that endurance sports are one of the mediums to deal with social stress. Endurance sports may bring together people with a shared interest as it builds more knowledge of those in the shared social network.

Endurance can help a teen girl who finds herself in a group of people with the same ideology to absorb all attitudes she might not be able to condone; she understands that humans are dynamic and may express themselves in ways that may not always be acceptable to others.

Due to pain, experience, or environment, some teen girls may find it difficult to mingle with their counterparts or peers. These may be in an academic setting, religious, or any activity they associate themselves with.

Studies have shown that this set of students tends to be passive most of the time because they may not find it easy to tolerate others.

Endurance may be an easy path for isolated teen girls to establish a quality network of friends as they tend to extend the passion that kept them going in such challenging tasks that gave them such virtues to the friends within the network.

Lastly, endurance generated through all rigorous activities that help her solve social stress bestows such a teen girl the prerequisite and know-how to manage every disheartening and frustrating behavior.

TIME

INTENSIVE SOLUTIONS:

Many social stressors involve complex and systemic issues that require time-intensive solutions. Endurance is essential for individuals and communities to stay committed to addressing these challenges despite setbacks and slow progress.

LEARNING

FROM SETBACKS:

Endurance involves learning from setbacks and using them as opportunities for growth. Social stress often comes with obstacles and setbacks, and building resilience through endurance allows individuals and communities to bounce back and persevere.

CULTURAL

AND STRUCTURAL CHANGE:

Achieving significant social change often involves challenging existing cultural norms and structural barriers. Endurance is critical for sustaining efforts over the long term and navigating the complexities of social transformation.

THE IMPORTANCE OF ENDURANCE IN SOLVING SOCIAL STRESS

NAVIGATING

INTERPERSONAL CHALLENGES:

Social stress can stem from interpersonal conflicts and challenges. Endurance is necessary for individuals to maintain relationships, work through conflicts, and foster understanding over time, even when faced with disagreements or misunderstandings.

SUSTAINED

ADVOCACY EFFORTS:

Social stressors may be addressed through advocacy and activism. Endurance is key for individuals and groups to sustain their efforts, whether it be advocating for social justice, equal rights, or policy changes.

BUILDING

COMMUNITY BONDS:

Endurance contributes to the building of strong community bonds. When individuals and communities persist in supporting each other through challenges, a sense of solidarity and collective strength is fostered, reducing the impact of social stressors.

CONCLUSION

This guide has established how teen girls need to reduce their anxiety levels as it has been able to educate and explain the effective strategies by which anxiety can be curbed or reduced. The guide, having followed many steps given by research works and numerous interviews with experts in the world of psychology and therapy alongside teenage girls, has been able to provide documented guides and techniques on how anxiety can be managed among teen girls.

A series of strategies can be followed to ensure anxiety among teen girls is appropriately reduced using some analytical description of instances gotten by some teens interviewed.

The guide also goes in-depth on how some teen girls develop anxiety from the academic environments and how well these anxieties and their prospects may be swiftly eliminated or, better still, redirected to a more positive measure.

It expands the horizon of the reader on the various means teen girls may be exposed to stress in school and how these pressures, if not cautiously attended to, may lead to the mental breakdown of the victims.

The beauty of this guide is numerous, and one of such insights that will propel the reader to read more is the well-detailed manner and comprehensive manner in which it is written. It is written in a language of easy comprehension that any person who gets in contact with it will not only find it an easy means of providing tips to issues relating to anxiety among teen girls but also will be able to practice the steps penned down due to its simple style of expression.

Furthermore, parents, caregivers, and teachers may teach teen girls some coping strategies to get the maximum results they anticipate.

As stated at the beginning of this guide's introduction, this is a complete work of research, interviews, and ideas garnered externally through various mediums and, therefore, is a subjective piece.

This guide has equally mentioned the prominent role of social networks and reduction in self-isolation as a probable measure towards addressing significant anxiety issues. It extends its message to how humans, especially teen girls, may use endurance garnered from various sources to solve social stress to the advantage of the body.

Therefore, teen girls should endeavor to take their time while studying this piece because it provides different techniques that can be applied to managing anxiety and converting a regular anxious person into a more relaxed mind.

Thanks for applying the coping strategies in this guide to your daily lives.

I tender a wealth of appreciation to every reader of this guide as it is quite educational with some attributes of illustrations given mostly by teen girls.